'In 2002 I was fired from my corporate job and forced to reinvent myself by starting my own business. It was really tough but after a long struggle it turned out to be the best career move I ever made.

I wish I had a copy of Ingrid's book fifteen years ago! I wouldn't have had as much difficulty getting going and I would have jumpstarted my business much faster.'

David Meerman Scott, bestselling author of ten books including *The New Rules of Marketing and PR*, now available in 29 languages from Albanian to Vietnamese.

'If the freedom and fun of starting your own business appeals, then do yourself a favour and follow Ingrid's proven seven step framework. Entrepreneurship is like a roller coaster ride, exhilarating yet terrifying, all at once. We're all nervous before we start, so allow Ingrid to guide you and she'll help you navigate the ups and downs!'

Adam Franklin, Best selling author of *Web Marketing That Works*

'I wish I had this book (and Ingrid!) when I started my business. It would have been such a huge help! Ingrid's experience and expertise shines as she outlines the 7 steps you must think about if you want to start a business. Read it now and you will be off to a great start!'

Louise Gooden, founder Mod. Financial Freedom

'Planning the start-up of your own business is an intense, amazing time, especially if you are doing this as you transition from a corporate career. Ingrid's 7-step guide and on-line tools are an investment you can't afford not to use – both as a structured planning checklist but also for Ingrid's personal insights and anecdotes which importantly highlight the emotional intelligence and resilience required.'

Christine Briggs, General Manager & Director, Australian manufacturing sector

T0098660

'If you are taking the brave step towards starting your very own business – who better to have by your side, than Ingrid Thompson.

Working with businesses of all types and sizes, Ingrid's reputation has grown over the years to become Australia's business start-ups authority.

Ingrid has an engaging style, mixing the facts with inspiring stories, as she expertly guides you through the complexities of starting a business, with perfectly placed activities to help break your journey into logical milestones.

With Ingrid's deep knowledge and expertise captured in her book 'So you want to start a business' – you will have everything you need to ensure you have all bases covered.'

Kathryn Williams, Your Financial Soul Mate®

'Starting a business is like jumping on a rollercoaster. Dizzying highs and terrifying lows. Having a resource that gives you the facts makes this ride a lot easier. These 7 steps don't need to be in any order and they are all important. If you are thinking about starting your own business then this book is for you.'

Jon Hollenberg, founder, Five by Five Web Design Agency

'If you want to know what works and how to do it, this book has the answers. Read it, follow it and get on your path!'

Robert Gerrish, founder Flying Solo, Australia's solo business community

'This awesome book by Ingrid really caught my eye. It's a world class book; a great book to give anyone you may know who is thinking of starting a business.'

Andrew Griffiths, bestselling author of 12 business books, global presenter, regular contributor to *Inc.*

SO YOU WANT TO START A BUSINESS

THE 7 STEP GUIDE

to Create Start & Grow Your Own Business

INGRID THOMPSON

NEW YORK

LONDON • NASHVILLE • MELBOURNE • VANCOUVER

SO YOU WANT TO START A BUSINESS

© 2018 Ingrid Thompson

Published in New York, New York, by Morgan James Publishing. Morgan James is a trademark of Morgan James, LLC.
www.MorganJamesPublishing.com

The Morgan James Speakers Group can bring authors to your live event. For more information or to book an event visit The Morgan James Speakers Group at www.TheMorganJamesSpeakersGroup.com.

ISBN 978-1-68350-743-7 paperback
ISBN 978-1-68350-744-4 eBook
Library of Congress Control Number: 2017913305

Cover Design by:
Rachel Lopez

Interior Design by:
Megan Whitney
Creative Ninja Designs
megan@creativeninjadesigns.com

In an effort to support local communities, raise awareness and funds, Morgan James Publishing donates a percentage of all book sales for the life of each book to Habitat for Humanity Peninsula and Greater Williamsburg.

Get involved today! Visit
www.MorganJamesBuilds.com

CONTENT

FOREWORD

I started my business the Australian Writers' Centre more than 10 years ago. I was clear from day one that it wasn't a side hobby. It was a serious business that I wanted to grow – and I knew I wanted to focus on providing the best writing courses in the country.

Not everyone is able to be this clear about what their business idea is and how to take their idea and create and start their own business. I meet a lot of people who are thinking about starting a business and I ask them: "What kind of business do you want to start?" and "Why do you want to start this business?" because these are the important questions. Many of the people I meet, especially in the tech start-up space, just want to find a business they can scale and sell.

Sometimes you can see they don't actually care about the business itself. It's really hard to sustain yourself in a business if you don't actually care about the product.

Today, more than ever, people dream about starting their own businesses, from young people choosing that option rather than work for someone else, to many women who are looking for a way to blend their professional expertise into a business that allows them to enjoy their family. And there are people in later stage of their careers looking for more meaningful expression of how they can create an income and lifestyle for themselves through starting a business of their own.

People of all ages are looking at how a business can be a viable alternative to working for someone else.

The truth is that success does not come easy in business. There are constant challenges and potentially multiple setbacks.

The pre-startup phase, the dreaming, idealistic and imaginative phase, is when you are the most excited and at the same time impatient; you just want to get going. You're eager to take your idea and run with it. This is the phase where good decision making is super important.

Because the idea generation phase is so exciting, any mention of "Planning" seems so stifling, limiting and constraining. And this is just what most "getting started in business" books are full of: business planning!

Ingrid Thompson has identified a gap in the market for a pre-startup book that isn't all about writing business plans. "So You Want to Start a Business" is a book that needed to be written and Ingrid is the perfect person to write it. Ingrid has successfully done what she suggests her readers do. This is a book that will help you decide many of the essential aspects of getting started in business.

Ingrid takes you, the reader, through the 7 steps to guide you in how to approach creating and starting your own business. She starts with "Who are You to start a business?" which is probably one of the most important chapters in the book. Who you are underpins your business success.

Each chapter is full of examples drawn from Ingrid's own 15 plus years of working in and around small businesses. Ingrid trained as an accountant and she brings a very practical and pragmatic approach to assist you with each aspect to create and start your own business. Her style is friendly and conversational. In fact, as I read sections of the book I could hear Ingrid's voice loud and clear.

Starting a business involves many steps. When you break it down and tackle it one little piece at a time, you do figure it out in the end. Ingrid has taken the complexity and set it out step by step. I suggest you take the time to read this book and complete all the exercises, activities and templates.

One of the greatest joys for me is to see people realise what they once thought was impossible. As you go through your business you will need different people at different times. Sometimes you might need a business coach, marketing experts, your lawyer, accountant.

At this pre-startup phase, you need Ingrid – and you need to read this book. I am confident that following the guidance offered in this book will see you business stand a greater chance of success.

Valerie Khoo

CEO, Australian Writers' Centre

WritersCentre.com.au

INTRODUCTION

*'The best time to plant a tree was twenty years ago.
The second best time is today.'*

CHINESE PROVERB

T here's never been a better time to start your own business.

The past fifty years has seen accelerated changes in how businesses operate and what it means to be in business. Many of us have seen a 'job for life' replaced by a 'portfolio career'. And, as we head towards the third decade of the 21st century, a new trend has emerged: entrepreneurs and startups. People are able to start their own business in addition to being a salaried employee, or even as an alternative to remaining an employee.

The new portfolio is much more extensive than merely moving from one job to another or changing job roles. The portfolio today looks more like a combination of any or all of the following:

- Running one's own entrepreneurial business
- Providing a service
- Creating a product
- Taking on a specific contract
- Engaging in part-time work as an employee.

These activities might all be taking place in parallel or in any combination across the months of a year. We have been hearing 'it's a changing landscape' since the 1990s; the changes that have caused the tectonic shifts in the way people work within large organisations are now the very changes that are enabling people to become entrepreneurs who start their own businesses.

TECHNOLOGY AND TRENDS

It would be easy to say technology has made the difference and, in many ways, it has. Much of the relevant technology is now free, or practically so, and its ready availability makes creating and growing a business easy. Technology allows us to create websites, leverage an e-commerce platform, track what our customers are buying, communicate through newsletters, blog, and set up social media profiles so that we can let our market know who we are, what we do and what we stand for.

Running your own business requires understanding a broad range of aspects. In the past, building knowledge and ongoing self-development meant going to night school or enrolling in a correspondence course. However, now, learning what to do and how to do it has never been easier. At the click of a mouse, we can find the solution to any problem. Whether through reading blogs, attending webinars or asking Google, we can learn about every aspect of business creation, all from the convenience of our home office.

Every day, there are new technologies available. Trying to keep up with everything can be like running a marathon with no finish line; however, there's no denying the opportunities these technologies provide. I personally love technology; I love that when Aung San Suu Kyi's only Sydney appearance was sold out, I could stand in my kitchen and watch the live stream from the Sydney Opera House on my iPad while making dinner, enjoying a glass of wine and tossing the cats' toy up the stairs. I love that I can Skype clients anywhere in the world and have conversations that are (almost) as intimate as if we were in the same room. I love that someone with a great idea can take that idea and, with the help of the available technology, create a business and life they love.

The new paradigm is down to more than just technological advances, however. There are other modern-day developments that mean there has never been a better time to become an entrepreneur and create a business. Let's look at a few of the other trending areas.

OUTSOURCING

There was a time when creating your own business meant that you did everything yourself or you employed someone full-time or part-time. You needed a physical place to work – an office, with a desk and computer – and your team, if you had one, would be based in the same place.

Again, thanks to technology, we now have access to skilled people who can work remotely, anywhere in the world. The person designing your logo could be in the next suburb, interstate or across the globe. Your virtual assistant can handle all your day-to-day matters from wherever they are located, whether next door or in another country. Rather than managing all the different departments required in your business, you can outsource activities to other businesses on a contract or piecemeal basis.

The effect is two-fold: on the one hand, this means it's easy to access the different skills and resources you need to build your business without hiring staff; and on the other, it means many more businesses out there are no longer constrained to manage every department in-house, and might be looking to source someone with your skillset and engage your business.

ACCEPTABILITY

Twenty years ago, it was rare to find someone saying they were starting their own business. They would, most likely, have been male and starting a plumbing or electrical business or other building-related business. They would have been giving it a go on their own after having completed their apprenticeship and having undertaken a few years working with an established business. Another example in the 1980s and 1990s was likely to be the man working in advertising who struck out on his own. Chefs and bakers may have ventured into their own business, too. And, in retail, a few designers created their own label and brand.

Around 2000, we saw a change, with large numbers of people made redundant from their corporate jobs. While many were forced into months of searching for another job, some brave souls opted for creating their own.

At about the same time, women were looking for ways to successfully combine family and work, and the idea of creating their own business was looking increasingly attractive. Instead of returning to a job in someone else's business, creating their own gave women what they needed – the flexibility to be available for children before and after school and at the same time have rewarding work in their chosen career or area of expertise.

Today, women are starting businesses at twice the rate of men. When someone says, 'I have my own business' it is now more likely to be met with, 'Of course!' rather than 'Oh, really?' It is so much more acceptable to be self-employed.

SECURITY

With the end of the 'job for life', there are many who believe that having one's own business offers greater security than working for someone else. Many find that having their own business gives them a greater sense of being in charge of their own destiny. This is especially true of a generation that has seen multiple cycles of redundancies, downsizings and (among the more honest) layoffs.

One of the advantages of setting up a business with solid foundations is that it can give you a level of security unlike any job. Being your own boss, working with your chosen clients and providing the level of service that you decide on can lead to greater security and financial rewards than may ever be experienced while working for someone else.

FINANCE

It has never been easier to find the funding to create a successful business. I remember attending a session about fifteen years ago where a business owner was describing the way investing in business was going to change. Her business was one of the new (at the time) Angel Investment businesses. An Angel Investment business is where successful entrepreneurs use their money to invest in new businesses to provide much needed funding to get them started. She helped match investors with people starting a business who needed funds. Often the money was invested as an 'Angel', meaning little or no involvement from the investing person.

Change really was coming. Over the past fifteen years, other new ways to raise funds have emerged, including crowd funding, self-funding and venture capital.

Even without outside funds, many people are able to create their own business today because it is easier and cheaper than ever to get set up. Ten years ago, a website could cost $20,000 – I had clients who paid that and more for their first websites! The same kind of website today would cost perhaps a quarter of that and, these days, many people are even setting up their first website for free. If you're selling a service and/or don't need up-front capital for inventory, your startup costs can be very low indeed.

We are living in a truly amazing time. There really has never been a better time to create your own business.

SO WHAT'S STOPPING YOU?

Are you thinking about creating a business of your own? Maybe you're an accountant who wants to create your own yoga school? Or a policewoman dreaming of opening your own flower shop? Perhaps you've completed your training as a physiotherapist, Pilates instructor or personal trainer, and you're currently working across a couple of different studios. Recently, you've found yourself wondering what it would be like to open your own. What if you could buy an established studio? Or create one from scratch? It would be nice to be your own boss, to have your own clients and to make all your own decisions. You find yourself wondering: what's involved? Where should you start?

Right now, whatever your skills, I'm guessing that you're an accomplished 'technician' and pretty good at what you do. Yet, when it comes to running a business:

- You don't know how to make money; you don't really understand finances and, if you're honest, you don't want to be stuck in the numbers – you'd rather be helping your clients.

- You have no plan, no roadmap, and you don't know how to make one.

- You aren't really sure how to find new clients. You know there's advertising and marketing and you've heard of SEO. Of course, everyone says you have to be on Instagram, Facebook and Twitter, and have a website. But you don't know how to sell yourself or leverage social media platforms.

- You're frightened of failing. What happens if it doesn't work? Will you look silly? Will people laugh at you? Will people say, 'I told you so...'? Could you potentially lose a lot of money?

- You don't really have any role models. While it seems just about everyone is starting a business, you don't personally know anyone who has done it. The television show Shark Tank is the closest thing you have to a mentor.

- Your friends and family are saying it would be better to get a good job or stay in your good job, and part of you believes they are right.

- So how can you overcome these hurdles and succeed beyond your wildest dreams? That's the purpose of this book.

You may have heard the statistic that says four out of every five startups fail. It can be a pretty scary prospect taking the leap when you think only one in every five people like you is successful at creating a business. My mission is to turn this around. At Healthy Numbers, we know how to help people create successful businesses. We know how to help get their heads out of the clouds, set their feet firmly on the ground and make their dream business a reality.

If you are reading this book, you likely already have an idea for your own business. If you follow the steps outlined in the following pages, you will end up with a business blueprint – a roadmap to follow when building your business. For the people who follow this system, I believe that we can change the success rate for startups. That's my mission – to change your chances of success to five out of five.

MY STORY

I started my first business in 2002 when I launched P'leisure Wear by Ingrid Louise. (You can check out my old website at www.ingridlouise.com.au). This business was somewhat successful, an important part of my entrepreneurial journey, and something I shall come back to later in this book. My current business, Healthy Numbers, came about by chance. In 2003, a friend asked me to come and help her niche training business. They needed a bookkeeper. I told her it had been years since I had done any accounting apart from the bookkeeping for my own business. 'You have to be better than the bookkeeper that we currently have,' she replied.

I accepted the challenge, dusted off my accounting books, enrolled in an MYOB course and fell in love with working with small businesses. This one client led to more clients, and through word-of-mouth, I created a startup whose goal was assisting small businesses to get their accounts in order. I developed a specialty for taking on businesses with extremely messy accounts, sorting through them and creating order, establishing systems and processes before handing the accounts back. It was an extremely satisfying and rewarding time in my business.

What I came to recognise during this time was the myriad of other challenges affecting small businesses. The business owners I worked with were always so busy building the business, looking for clients, and creating products and services, that it was easy to neglect accounting, bookkeeping, and the processes and systems that were an integral part of running the business well.

In many cases, the business owner was extremely good at what they did. They had just never been taught any kind of business acumen. I knew this was something that I could help them with. And I could help others earlier in the process. What if we helped people to understand what is involved in creating, starting and running a business *before* they actually started their business? I thought about my corporate training days when we would provide supervisor, team-leader and manager training to aspiring leaders before they moved into a leadership role. They would have the opportunity to act in the role and build on their skills before they actually moved into a full-time management position.

I decided to do the same for people aspiring to start their own business – teach them the business acumen that is as necessary for running their business as their technical training. This would set solid foundations and provide better opportunity for business success.

Fast forward to the present day and I've worked with almost 1,000 businesses at different stages in their business evolution. I have provided clients with business coaching and training in business basics to help them understand what it takes to create their own business. And I have set countless entrepreneurs up for success when it comes to running those businesses. The reason I know what you are thinking and the questions you have is because I've worked with many people just like you. Smart. Caring. Kind. Generous. Wanting to make a difference. Wanting to create a business that will give you the lifestyle that you want for yourself and your family.

I've helped people build their own sustainable business in order to create a rewarding income and lifestyle for themselves and their families – I call this a Lifestyle Business. And I've helped dozens of people go from solo operator to running organisations making six figures – those who want to build a Big Business. Over the years, I have even prevented a few businesses from going bankrupt, protecting them from the heartbreak of losing everything. What I've learned from working with so many business startups is that people need a formula to follow.

STARTING YOUR BUSINESS: SEVEN ESSENTIAL ELEMENTS

It doesn't really matter what sort of business you are starting, there are certain things that every would-be business owner needs to do to get started. The chapters in this book explain the process I follow with my clients. There are seven essential elements involved in starting a successful business, which I outline here.

1. YOU

Your business starts with you. Who are you to start a business? Some people are more suited to starting a business than others, and in this part of the book, we explore what it takes to be a business person. There are two key questions when it comes to starting a business:

- Do you know what you're getting yourself into?
- And are you truly capable of it?

I show you what it really takes to run your own business and what you need to learn.

2. YOUR IDEA

In this chapter, we answer some important questions about the keystone of your startup. What is your business idea? Who really wants it? Is it better than what is currently available? What problem does it solve? Understanding the competition is important at this stage; most startups are surprised when they begin investigating the range of both direct and indirect competition in the marketplace. In this part of the book, I show you how to identify your point of difference and claim your niche. Ultimately, you need to know: is your business idea viable? Are there people out there who want what you offer and are prepared to pay money for it?

3. YOUR CLIENTS

Who, in fact, is your ideal client? What do you know about them and what do you *need* to know about them? In this chapter, we use a framework to understand the various aspects involved. This will help you to create an ideal client avatar. We dig deep in order to understand the real value that you provide for them, as well as considering how and where you will find them.

4. YOUR BRAND

It can be easy to think that branding is only for the big guys. However, for a small startup, defining your brand is just as important, if not more so. Your brand is your story. Your clients are looking to you to stand for something. This is one of the strengths of a small business: you get to say what is important to you personally, and your clients can connect with that on a more intimate level than is possible with a huge enterprise. In this part of the book, we look at brand awareness and promotion.

5. YOUR STRUCTURE

When you start a business, there are compliance matters and legalities to adhere to. It's important to stay on the right side of the law and to set solid foundations for your business. In this chapter, we look at the legal structure of your business and set out the pros and cons of the different structures available. We look at insurance, risk management, and systems and processes. We also take a look at your support team and consider how to surround yourself with the best people.

6. YOUR FINANCES

Over time, I've found that many of the people who wish to start their own business are not really numbers people. How much will it cost to get started? Where will the money come from? When you are running a business, it is important to understand some of the financial basics: the difference between revenue and profit; how to calculate whether you are making a profit or a loss; how to manage cash flow; what prices to charge; and more. I specialise in making numbers easy to understand (some have even called me a 'numbers whisperer'), and that's the aim in this part of the book.

7. YOUR MARKETING

Marketing is all about attracting and retaining clients. In this part of the book, we create a client journey map that will help you identify the various points of contact where your clients interact with your business. I like to think of them as moments of truth. Advertising and social media are important elements for communicating with your clients, and the available technology is constantly changing. However, your underpinning philosophy is driven by your values, which are more constant. No matter what medium you are using, there are fundamentals that bring clients to your business and then keep them coming back. Taking the time to develop your marketing plan will contribute to your chances of success.

Throughout this book, there are a series of activities for you to help you prepare for setting up your business. We know that some people like to work with pen and paper, on separate sheets of paper or in a dedicated notebook. Others prefer to work on their iPad or computer. Please do what works for you. The important thing is to consider and complete the activities and to keep them all in one place for easy reference.

The book is written in an order purely based on the way I work with my clients. You might prefer to jump ahead to a chapter you are particularly interested in and then jump back. That will work just fine for some people, just as starting at the beginning and following the elements in their order will be effective for others. However, I would suggest going through the first chapter – the one about you – first. And, in whatever order, every business startup needs to address every essential element. You're not doing yourself any favours if you skip the chapters you're not comfortable with (people who hate numbers, I'm looking at you!).

Once you have your blueprint in place, it's up to you to run with it. Being in business can be crazy, but it can be good crazy! Working through this process and reaching this point will instil you with confidence when it comes to your business idea and your business plan. You'll know you're on track to build the business that will give you the life you want. Then, all you need to do is start running it!

Do you remember going to the beach as a child and testing the waters? Starting a business is like heading into the surf on your own for the first time. You may be a confident swimmer, but you're nervous and excited at the same time. You're standing on the beach, watching the waves, and trying to judge which ones you can jump into, which ones you should jump over, and which are best to avoid altogether. This book will help you tell the difference and enjoy the experience without any mishaps. Think of me as your swim coach and lifeguard combined.

Are you ready? Let's go!

1. YOU

'I wake up every morning thinking … this is my last day. And I jam everything into it. There's no time for mediocrity. This is no damned dress rehearsal.'

ANITA RODDICK

You're enjoying Friday night drinks after a difficult week and someone says, 'We should start our own business. We're the brains here. If we worked this hard for ourselves, imagine how much money we would make!'

The next morning, at your Pilates class, you just can't shake the idea. As you head to the coffee shop across the road for breakfast, you wonder if it just might be possible.

You think about the other people who have created their own businesses and consider what they have … Success. Flexibility. Creative freedom. Fulfilment. They are their own boss. They make a difference, while living their dream. People respect them for what they have achieved. By the time you've finished breakfast and are walking home, the creative ideas are flowing and you can imagine all of this for yourself.

And, then, there she is – that little voice inside your head that asks you all the really difficult questions and discourages you from doing what you want. (Call me nuts, but I named mine Natalie. I find it helps to separate myself from her – it gives her less power over my thoughts and my actions.)

Natalie's talking in that tone of voice that lets you know she thinks you're crazy ... 'What do you know about running a business? And, anyway, what sort of business would you start?' She plants a huge seed of doubt in your mind. You think, 'Yeah, who am I to start a business? It was different for all of the others. They probably had loads of help, lots of money and already knew people. It's a nice dream, but it could never really happen ...'

Or could it?

In this part of the book, we are going to humour Natalie and play devil's advocate, but in the process, we're going to help you get really clear on what you want and whether you have what it takes to achieve it. What does it take to be someone who creates a business and life they love? What makes people who start their own businesses different to other people? What are some of the key characteristics of people who create successful businesses?

Today, people are creating businesses more than at any other time in history. Setting the right foundations will put you on track to join the others who have become enormously successful. They all had to start somewhere – just like you.

Faced with a decision, we can feel stuck at a crossroads – we have the choice to go somewhere we have been before, where it is familiar, comfortable, easier. And we have the choice to step up to a new level. What stops many people is an inner glass ceiling. But this ceiling is self-imposed. Letting it stop you is self-sabotage.

By the end of this chapter, you will have clarity about what you really want and what it takes to start a business. I will challenge you to commit to the process or decide it truly isn't for you – but based on a strong, hard look at yourself and what you want to achieve rather than baseless feelings that you couldn't do it even if you tried. If you really want to learn, you can do anything! Complete the activities under each section and unleash your inner entrepreneur.

ARE YOU ESCAPING FROM OR MOVING TOWARDS?

In the 1100s, in the remote mountains of northern Europe, there stood a walled village with a gatekeeper. Along the road came a man and his family.

On approach, the man called, 'Good gatekeeper, hello and fine day,' to which the gatekeeper replied, 'Hello and fine day to you, good fellow.'

'Good gatekeeper, we have travelled far looking to make our home in a new village. What kind of people live in your village?'

'Tell me, good fellow,' said the gatekeeper, 'what kind of people did you find in your last village?'

'Good gatekeeper, the village we have left behind is filled with scoundrels and thieves.'

The gatekeeper shook his head. 'Good fellow, you will find that this village is also filled with scoundrels and thieves.'

So the man and his family bid the gatekeeper, 'Fond farewell,' and continued on along the road.

By and by, another man and his family came along the same road and, on approach, the man called to the gatekeeper, 'Good gatekeeper, hello and fine day,' to which the gatekeeper replied, 'Hello and fine day to you, good fellow.'

'Good gatekeeper, we have travelled far looking to make a home in a new village. What kind of people live in your village?'

'Tell me, good fellow,' said the gatekeeper, 'what kind of people were in your last village?'

'Good gatekeeper, the village we have left behind is filled with people generous and friendly. The salt of the earth.'

The gatekeeper smiled. 'Good fellow, you will find that this village is also filled with people who are generous and friendly. The salt of the earth.'

I love this story because it illustrates how we create our own world in so many ways. How often do we hear of someone who has to move house because they have the "neighbours from hell"? They move, only to find themselves living next to another set of neighbours from hell. Or what about that person we know who has to leave their job because it's so awful? They escape the job they hate, only to find themselves signing up for an equally awful job. They leave behind one overly controlling manager, only to find themselves working for an equally or even more controlling manager.

When considering starting your own business, there are two important questions:

- What are you escaping from?
- What are you moving towards?

For many people, the answers to these questions are intrinsically linked. You might be escaping from the regimen of having to be at a desk, having to be in the workplace at 8:30am on the dot, having to work long hours, having to meet other people's expectations, and still feeling like nothing you do really matters.

You might be moving towards having the flexibility to work at 10pm at night or 4pm in the afternoon if that is what works for you, having the need to work like crazy only when you want to meet a deadline, and having the option to go for a surf or attend a morning yoga class whenever you want – every day if you want!

Activity: Escaping From and Moving Towards

Take the time now to think about both questions – what are you escaping from and what are you moving towards? Use two pages in your notebook and write one question at the top of one page, the other question at the top of the other. Take the first question and set a timer for five minutes. Write down as many answers as you can – list all the things that you believe you are escaping from. When the timer goes off, set question one to one side.

Stand up and stretch – forward, back and side to side. Go for a short walk or skip around the room or do twenty star jumps. Maybe drink a glass of water.

Take the second page with question two at the top and set your timer for five minutes. Write down as many answers as you can – list all the things that you believe you are moving towards.

When the timer goes off, leave that page aside and again stand up and stretch. Go for a walk or do some star jumps.

This activity aims to get you thinking about why you want to take this step. Starting your own business is a big decision. In the next couple of sections, we are going to look into this further.

LIVING THE DREAM, BUT WHOSE DREAM?

When I was in my late teens, a friend invited me to attend a self-development weekend. It was held in one of those lovely, peaceful settings, with trees and birds and fresh air. We shared in helping prepare the meals and other tasks. Everyone was quietly-spoken and smiled a lot. There was designated time for meditation and yoga, and lots of walks into spectacular Australian bush, with stunning views looking down onto the tops of massive eucalyptus gum trees.

There was a moment that stood out for me in one of the sessions with one of the speakers, Midge. She described the 'Happy when …' way of living and gave examples of the way many people live in this way. She described how people go through life saying:

- 'I'll be happy when … I finish school'

- 'I'll be happy when … I have a boyfriend'

- 'I'll be happy when … we get engaged'

- 'I'll be happy when … we are married'

- 'I'll be happy when … I get a promotion'

- 'I'll be happy when … we find the right house'

- 'I'll be happy when … the house has a lovely garden'

- 'I'll be happy when … I get a pay rise'

- 'I'll be happy when … we have a baby'

- 'I'll be happy when … we have a second child'

- 'I'll be happy when … the children go to school'

- 'I'll be happy when ... the children get to high school'

- 'I'll be happy when ... I can retire'

And so the list goes on ...

For many people, living in this perpetual anticipation of future happiness that is based on some future event, it turns out that these aren't even their own dreams. They often aren't living their own story. They are chasing goals that were important to their parents' notions of happiness, or are important to their partner or peers.

Why do people get caught up allowing other people to decide when they'll be happy? Apart from anything else, it stops people from believing that they can be happy *now*.

Intrigued at the notion that people live in this future 'Happy when ...' way, I decided to research and explore the idea further. I focussed on listening to how people talked about their lives, listening for the 'Happy when ...' stories. I encountered many people living with this mindset. And as I listened carefully, it seemed true that, for many, the 'I'll be happy when ...' stories were not their own. They were often the dreams of parents, husbands, wives, colleagues or bosses.

Of course, the big question is: how is this useful?

It's obvious that having a desired future dream, which is different to our current situation, can be useful in helping us decide what to do on a daily basis. *I'm here, but I want to be there. What do I need to do to get there?*

You may recognise this as the foundation of goal setting. Current position; future desire; action plan. The thing that Midge helped me understand, however, is how important it is to make sure the dreams you have are your own. Otherwise, when you get there, you realise you're still not happy; so you just progress to the next 'Happy when ...' and never achieve the anticipated happiness.

Over the years, I have worked with hundreds of people to help them understand three simple things:

- Where are you now?

- Where do you want to go?

- What do you need to do to get there?

The key to this is **you**. It is about where *you* want to go and what *you* need to do to get there.

One of my favourite examples is Chris Hadfield, a Canadian who, at the age of nine, decided he wanted to be an astronaut. It was very much *his* dream. At the time, Canada didn't have a space program. However, Chris knew it was what he wanted for the future, so every day and in every situation, he asked himself, 'What would an astronaut do?' He even asked himself, 'Would an astronaut eat green vegetables or fast food?' And so he ate his green vegetables and carried on asking himself the question every day, until, eventually, when Canada posted an advert looking for their first astronaut, Chris Hadfield had every attribute necessary to apply. He was one of five chosen from 5,000 applicants and went on to travel to space multiple times.

You need to ask yourself the same questions. Not necessarily 'What would an astronaut do?' but:

- Where am I now?

- Where do I want to go?

- What do I need to do to get there?

Creating your own business is only one aspect of your overall life. However, you have a dream for what you want your life to be and creating your own business may well offer you the means by which you are able to create more of what you want in other aspects of your life. It's important to understand how creating your own business will contribute to giving you the life you love today and in the future.

DOONA DAYS: PROS AND CONS

In Australia, your doona is what you call your duvet or comforter. Some days, you just want to stay under the covers, and I'm having one of those days right now! Today has been allocated to writing my book, but I truly would rather be doing anything else – surfing, swimming, walking in the park, sitting in the garden, reading a book, watching a movie, even vacuuming the house!

It feels like it has been a long week. I've been working with several new clients, each of whom has required significant amounts of time and energy. We're going through all the aspects of their businesses and generating action plans for improving things. At the same time, I've been working with two clients who are about to lose their businesses. We are exploring the best way for the businesses to close, wind up or be sold. I've also spent two full days training people in leadership and team skills. It's no wonder I want to take the day off and write this book another day.

But will this book write itself? No way! Not unless I outsource it to a ghost writer, but that's not something I want to do because I'm so passionate about this topic. I want to be the one to make a difference for the people who read these words, and help them create businesses that give them lives they love.

So what do I do to get myself in the mood and back on track? I've already started to feel better just writing that last paragraph – it's a solid reminder of why I'm here.

There are days I need to remind myself why I am doing this, why I am in my business and why I am writing this book. There are going to be days when you feel the same. Sometimes, when we're in a job, working for an employer, we can call in sick or have a slow day. In fact, some companies actually have official, designated doona days, not quite the same as a sick day, but allowing an employee who really doesn't feel like showing up to take the day off. Of course, there are limits to how many of these any one individual can take before their boss wants to have a chat with them.

Maybe, when you start your business, you can set yourself up with a certain number of doona days –flexible days that allow you to put off doing what you know needs to be done, or to work on activities that allow you to get back in the mood. However, the reality is, you probably won't have this luxury. Chances are, especially at the beginning, your business will require 100 per cent of your attention, seven days a week.

I don't have a doona day allowance in my business ... so here I am, tapping away. I've chosen to write this chapter because if this doesn't inspire me, what will? One of the key ways to get through the doona days is to remind yourself why you are doing what you are doing.

So why *are* you creating your business?

THE PROS OF CREATING YOUR OWN BUSINESS

As we've discussed, there has never been a better time to create your own business. In this book's Introduction we covered the global and societal reasons, such as new technology and reduced barriers to entry. Now, this section focuses on you and your individual reasons. These will provide the inspiration to keep going on days when you just don't want to carry on.

I'm an unashamed 'pros and cons' person. When facing decisions, I get out my paper and pen and write my lists for and against.

When I ask people, 'What are the pros and cons of creating your own business?' there is such a variety of responses. This is the one part of creating your business where there really is no right or wrong answer. Something that is a pro for one person might be a con for another.

Activity: Pros

Take out your notebook and set a timer for five minutes.

Write down all the pros of creating your own business. No filtering or justifying or rationalising. Record your pure thoughts about what you see as the pluses, the positives. These are the reasons for creating your own business.

Over the years, I have given this exercise to clients and participants in training sessions. There is no absolute list, though I have observed certain themes and similarities showing up.

Being my own boss tops the list for many people. While it can have different meanings for different people, it's generally not about sitting with your feet on the desk barking orders at the underlings. It's about having autonomy. This filters down into all of the points below.

DECISION-MAKING

Making your own decisions can apply to a range of areas, including:

- Choosing the clients you want to work with.

- How you define customer service and create and build client relationships.

- How you build relationships with partners/suppliers.

- How you define the levels of service you deliver and who receives which levels of service.

- Selecting which products you offer.

- Designing the systems and processes you use.

- Establishing your own boundaries.

- Creating your own work environment.

TIME MANAGEMENT

For many people, this is a key benefit. Having your own business allows you to:

- Work around doing the things that you enjoy.

- Work around the needs of your family and other responsibilities.

- Work from home and avoid commuting.

- Work to your own self-imposed deadlines.

CREATIVE FREEDOM

This is an important positive and manifests differently. It can refer to:

- Making a living from something you love.

- Making a living doing something you are skilled at.

- Creating products that are beautiful.

- Listening to what clients want and creating products and services that meet clients' needs.

- Being able to use your imagination.

- Bringing passion and vitality to your business.

MAKING A DIFFERENCE

This is another pro that tops many people's list. It can include:

- Making a difference for clients.

- Making a difference for the community.

- Creating a business that employs people.

- Creating a business that trains people.

- Creating something that has a higher purpose.

- Feeling like your efforts count for something, and contribute to something.

CONTROLLING YOUR OWN FUTURE

Again, this can encompass different things:

- Financial freedom.

- Having the opportunity to create and grow something different.

- Generating income without trading your time for money.

- Embracing new challenges.

- Having room for growth/personal development.

- Never being bored again.

It's not all roses, however. You have to look at the cons, and decide whether your pros make all the hard work worth it.

THE CONS OF CREATING YOUR OWN BUSINESS

As much as there are lots of terrific, positive reasons for starting your own business, there are also downsides. For every up, there is a down.

Activity: Cons

Let's go back to your notebook and set the timer for another five minutes.

Write down all the cons of creating your own business. Again, no filtering or justifying or rationalising. Just record your pure thoughts about what you see as the downsides to creating your own business. These are all the reasons not to.

When you look at what you have written on each list, you may find some of the same points. For many people, *being my own boss and responsible for my own future* also tops their list of cons. An upside can also be a downside. You might think, 'Yay, I'm totally responsible,' but at the same time, 'Being responsible is scary.'

Here are some of the cons of creating your own business that I've heard over the years. The thing is, a lot of these issues can be addressed. Many of them I specifically address in this book, so I've included the reference.

No Sick Pay and No Holiday Pay

When you work as an employee for someone else, it can feel like they are paying you for doing nothing when you are on annual leave or sick leave. It feels like a bonus and a security blanket. However, it's important to remember that they have factored the cost of paying your holidays into your total salary package. In the same way, you can factor the cost of your leave into your pricing (refer to the section in Chapter 6: Pricing).

Not Having Anyone to Fall Back On or Push You

Indeed. You will be a 'one-man (or woman) band'. This is why it is critical to build a support team around you, even if it's not in the traditional sense (refer to the section in Chapter 5: The Power of a support team).

High Competition

You're going to have competition every step of the way. And there's even a risk that others will copy your ideas. You'll constantly need to find new ways to offer your products and services. It's possible, however, to embed strategies and tactics into your business practices to ensure that you're always attractive to your clients (refer to the section in Chapter 2: Is your idea better than the rest?).

Sales

Having to sell yourself is one of the key issues that people face when they create their own business. However, knowing your value proposition and being really clear about your niche is a great start (refer to the section in Chapter 2: Is your idea better than the rest?), and there are ways to outsource some of the selling aspects of business to your support team (refer to the section in Chapter 5: The power of a support team).

Getting Clients to Pay Their Accounts and Pay On Time

Often, people are drawn to create a business by a desire to help others. It's easy to feel uncomfortable asking for and chasing payments. Working on developing a business mindset helps (refer to the section coming up in Chapter 1: Do you have a business mindset?).

Other Money Matters

Taxes are a particularly pesky component of this. And, yes, you will need to know the basics. Developing a business mindset (refer to the section coming up in Chapter 1: Do you have a business mindset?), and getting a good accountant and bookkeeper will help keep you on track (refer to the sections in Chapter 6: Taxes, and Keeping up with your financials). Keeping pace with how much money is in the bank is another issue. You will think about money more in your own business than you ever did when you were an employee in someone else's business. But this can be a good thing (we look at cash flow in Chapter 6: Managing cash flow).

Compliance

Knowing the rules and legislation about hiring and employing employees can be onerous, though having a great Human Resources partner can ensure you are fully compliant (refer to the section in Chapter 5: The power of a support team). Meanwhile, you also have to know about insurance, permits, licences and staying on the right side of the law. There are ways to check you are compliant with any regulations (refer to the section in Chapter 5: Compliance matters), but whichever way you look at it, there's a lot to keep an eye on.

So, if there are so many downsides, why on earth do people continue to start businesses? This is a terrific question, but it has an answer. Sometimes, the force pushing you towards starting a business is greater than the force holding you back from starting a business.

DOONA DAYS: YOUR 'WHY'

Your 'why' is your underpinning philosophy. It encompasses your purpose and values. This is the force that is driving you to start your business, in spite of the challenges. It's the real reason to get out from under the doona!

In his book *Start with Why*, Simon Sinek offers interesting insight into why some organisations achieve high levels of success and exceptional degrees of influence. He describes the Golden Circle as the What, the How and the Why of business.

The example that Simon Sinek uses in his famous TED Talk is Apple. If Apple were a traditional computer company, it might say, 'We make great computers, they're beautifully designed, simple to use and user friendly.' Usually, a company says what it does: 'We make great computers,' and then says how they are different: 'The computers are beautifully designed, simple to use and user friendly.' They finish with: 'Please buy my computer.' You can watch the TED Talk here: https://www.ted.com/talks/simon_sinek_how_great_leaders_inspire_action

Instead, what Apple does is start with its 'why': 'Everything we do, we believe in challenging the status quo. We believe in thinking differently.' Then Apple says 'how' it does this: 'The way we challenge the status quo by making products that are beautifully designed, simple to use and user friendly.' And, finally, 'what' Apple does: 'We just happen to make computers ... Do you want to buy one?'

I do a lot of work with Pilates and yoga instructors. One of my clients wants to change the way people use their bodies every day and create healthier communities – this is her why. How she does it is by helping people stand taller, gain strength and sleep better. She just happens to teach Pilates; do you want to book a session?

Let's take a closer look at the components of the Golden Circle.

WHAT

This relates to the job title, the technical skill, the products and/or the services that you sell. Every organisation on the planet knows what they do, whether they are a large company or a small business, irrespective of industry. Ask anyone working in any business and they can tell you what they do. *What* is easy to identify.

HOW

This can set a business apart from the competition. This is how the business does what it does. *How* is often used to explain in what way something is different or better. It can be articulated through consideration of your values.

Values are important and lasting beliefs or ideals about what is good or bad. They serve as guidelines for our behaviour. Values can become the standards by which people make choices and live their lives.

A couple of years ago, I was working with a young couple running a dental practice. They had a strong philosophy. It was one of their values to treat everyone who came into the practice with high regard. Everyone knew what this meant and they lived it every day.

When the computer and phone system started playing up, they called in the local IT expert. After a few weeks full of frustrating moments, the systems were all working perfectly again, and the IT expert said, 'I'd like to make a booking to come to see this dentist.' They were a bit surprised because, at some point, he had mentioned that he went to another dentist in town. But he continued, 'In twenty or so years of going to my other dentist, I have always been treated just like any other patient. Every time I come in here, you are all so nice, and nice to me – even though I'm just the IT guy. I have seen you at some of the most frustrating times in the past few weeks and you still behave the same. I want to come back here. It feels good.'

When my client told me this story, they were very proud of their team for being able to live one of their core values and treat everyone with high regard. That was a strong part of how they ran their business.

It's easy for some in business to believe that *how* is the differentiating factor, but there's one more part ...

WHY

Why do people do what they do? Why does their business exist? Very few people and fewer businesses are able to clearly articulate why they do what they do. Those that can do this successfully truly differentiate themselves from the rest. Some would argue that the business exists to make money, but making money is actually the result of what you do. Why you do it is your purpose, your cause – your belief.

As Sinek says, 'People don't buy what you do. They buy **why** you do it.' Understanding your beliefs and knowing your 'why' is the first step to creating the foundations for your business.

When I think of the dentist I mentioned earlier, he had a very strong 'why'. He had a vision of a world where patients' knowledge and understanding of preventative dental hygiene would mean his role as a dentist could be made redundant – it would no longer be necessary.

When you set up a small business, there is going to be loads of competition. Being very clear and specific about the reason you do what you do – being able to communicate your strong 'why' – will set you apart from everyone else.

It's also what will keep you going on the doona days, when you really wonder if you can continue another minute. You can come back to your 'why' and that will give you the strength, fortitude and tenacity to continue. Over and over, when I speak with people in their own businesses, they tell me that being very clear about their beliefs, their values and their 'why' is what gives them the strength to keep going when things get tough.

Activity: Your Golden Circle

Get out your notebook and start with why.

Why: Why do you do what you do? What do you believe? This is your purpose – it sits on a higher level than what your business will do or make. It can be helpful to start writing notes beginning: 'I believe ...' or 'I envisage a world ...'

When you put pen to paper, you'll be surprised at what comes. Your finished statement will be about two lines long – no more – and it will describe what you believe and/or the value you and your business provide to the world. It won't necessarily mention your product or your service.

How: Explain how you think and how you act. You'll probably have about three to five distinct values or characteristics that differentiate you and your business. These make you unique in the way you go about achieving your vision. Businesses that do this well have specific and actionable ideas so that everyone can be held accountable.

I recently met Naomi Simson, the founder of a business called Red Balloon. She told me that one of Red Balloon's values is about always being totally customer-centric. In the early days of running her business, which was in the early 2000s, she personally called every single customer to ask about their experience using Red Balloon. In another example, Gary Nicholls, who created an online business selling clotheslines, would send every single customer a handwritten thank you card in the mail after making their purchase. I even worked with a dentist who used to make her own care calls, the day after a patient had been in for treatment, despite such calls usually being made by a member of the practice team. Each of these examples shows the business owner's values in action.

You'll find a core values worksheet at: http://www.healthynumbers. com.au/book-templates/. This is a list that you can work through to identify your top three to five values. Put this into a statement, and you have your how!

What: This is your idea – what you're intending to do or provide. We're going to test this idea in the next part of the book.

Here are the elements of my own Golden Circle, tied together in my vision statement:

I inspire individuals to create a successful business in order to give them the life they desire. In everything I do to bring this vision into reality, I hold myself accountable to my five guiding principles:

1. **Keep it simple:** When someone understands something, it's more likely to be achieved.

2. **Take action:** Prolific beats perfect every time.

3. **Look for the good:** There's as much benefit in recognising where things are working and building on that, as focusing on fixing what isn't working.

4. **Tell the truth:** Sometimes, people get so close to their ideas that they cannot see the 'forest for the trees'. It's best to be really honest with people preparing to start a business. This can help them avoid costly mistakes, both financial and emotional.

5. **Collaborate:** Work with others. Ask for help from those who know and those who have been there already.

So what do I, Ingrid, do? In a world where there is a gap between what people need to know and what the traditional education system continues to teach, I write about the important elements involved in establishing a successful business. I share information that will inspire individuals to ask the difficult questions when getting started. I personally ask as many questions as possible of people who I think may know the answers. And I work to be my own best business case study, practising everything I tell and show others.

DO YOU HAVE WHAT IT TAKES?

So we've looked at what you want and what's driving you. Now, there are a few important questions to ask yourself. Even better, find a neutral party, someone you don't already know, like a business coach or business consultant, to ask you.

Here are fifteen of the questions I find it most helpful to ask my clients:

1. DO YOU LIKE TO PLAN?

The answer needs to be 'yes'. There are a lot of things that you will need to organise: a business plan, marketing plan, growth plan and exit plan, to name a few. You will be able to outsource some aspects of your business (we'll talk more about outsourcing later), but there'll always be an element of planning!

2. ARE YOU ABLE TO ORGANISE YOUR TIME?

Again, you need to answer 'yes'. When you start out as a solopreneur, you will wear all the hats: Chief Executive Officer (CEO), Chief Financial Officer (CFO), Chief Operations Officer (COO), Sales Manager, Marketing Manager, Accounts, Dispatch, and so it goes on.

I remember meeting Peter Alexander, the founder of Peter Alexander sleepwear. He told me the story about his early days in business, when it was just himself and his mother. They used to answer the phone with different voices. "Hello, Barbara in Dispatch ... okay, I'll put you through to Sally in Accounts ...' New voice: 'Hello, Sally in Accounts ... I'll put you through to our Sales Department ...' New voice: 'Natalie in Sales here ...' They developed the characters so they always knew who they were. Reflecting on this story it's interesting to wonder if today, Peter would feel the need to create this charade. Today many clients and customers enjoy knowing they are working with a bespoke business and that they deal personally with the owner and founder.

Eventually, you will have other people to help you, but you will still need to be organised. One of the key balancing acts that new business owners need to master is doing the work and at the same time looking for new clients and customers; you are responsible not only for production, but sales and business growth.

3. HOW WELL DO YOU DISTANCE YOURSELF FROM WHAT OTHERS THINK ABOUT YOU?

Years ago, I heard Dr Phil McGraw talking on the Oprah show about this topic and he referred to advice that his dad had given him: 'Phil, people aren't thinking about you as much as you think they are.' This echoes an Eleanor Roosevelt quote: 'You wouldn't worry so much about what others think of you if you realised how seldom they do.' Pretty much most people are actually thinking about themselves.

If you feel a bit miffed by this, think of it as liberating, as a type of freedom. So often, people are held back by concern about what others will think. But if you want to start a business, you have to go for it full-heartedly – don't let others hold you back. Give yourself a good talking to and remind yourself that people most likely aren't thinking about you at all. Which leads me to self-talk ...

4. CAN YOU CONTROL YOUR SELF-TALK?

There will be the voice that tells you, 'Keep doing what you're doing! This business is a fabulous success,' and then there will be the voice that says, 'Who do you think you are? Just look at this disaster happening here.'

Are you able to deal with this second voice? I already mentioned my first technique, which has been to name her Natalie, separating her from me so as to give her less power over me. When she starts to speak, I greet her mentally. 'Oh, hello, Natalie!' Then, I challenge her language. So when she says, 'This is a disaster,' I reply, 'Disaster? Really? No, not a disaster. It might be a bit inconvenient right now, but there is a way to solve it.' I find that challenging overly-dramatic language works, more often than not. A disaster is when your children are swept out to sea, your dog is run over on the road, and so on. When a client doesn't buy your stuff, that's disappointing, not a disaster! Whatever happens in business, there's a solution.

5. ARE YOU WILLING TO TRY OUT NEW IDEAS? AND TAKE RISKS?

If you are serious about creating your own business, this has to be a definite 'yes'. Every part of what you are doing involves risk and the need to embrace new ways of thinking and new ideas. Knowing the difference between a reckless risk and a calculated risk is important. Mitigating or reducing the potential impact of calculated risks is what business owners do every day.

6. ARE YOU TENACIOUS?

This question's a bit different – we want the answer to be 'yes' and 'no'. Yes, you need to be tenacious in order to hang in there for the long haul – so you keep moving towards your goal and stick with it. Having a clear vision, your values and a sense of why you are in business, as well as having a strong team around you, will support your ability to be tenacious. There are numerous examples of tenacity in the history of startups. Who would have thought in 1999 that the tenacity of Larry Page and Sergy Brin would see Google unseat Yahoo? The terrific movie *Joy* (2015), based on the life of Joy Mangano (played by Jennifer Lawrence), demonstrates the tenacity necessary in business. Joy has an idea for a miracle mop and overcomes many hurdles to bring her mop to market.

There may be times, however, when being tenacious would be a disadvantage. For example, holding on to something that is truly not going to work, and holding on for too long.

7. ARE YOU RESILIENT?

Resilience is different to tenacity. Resilience refers more to 'bounce-back-ability' – the ability to bounce back when things go wrong, when ideas fail or when disappointments occur. A big part of building resilience in business is not taking matters personally. How many editors said 'no' to J K Rowling before one accepted the Harry Potter series? And one of my favourite examples of resilience is Malala Yousafzai, who said, 'I don't want to be remembered as the girl who was shot. I want to be remembered as the girl who stood up.' (*Huffington Post*, September 2013)

8. ARE YOU OPTIMISTIC? DO YOU SEE THE GLASS AS HALF FULL?

There may be days when the phone doesn't ring, when no one will answer your calls, when people avoid you, when there are no emails, and no customers walk through the door. Being able to recognise that the past is not the future is key. You need to see opportunities where others might not. You need to take what is happening and 'turn it to good'. Ask, 'What can I learn here?' and 'What needs to change so that what's happening doesn't continue?' You need to recognise that it's all part of the business journey and not lose faith.

9. DO YOU HAVE PASSION FOR YOUR BUSINESS?

Passion is important. But I'm not talking about being a dewy-eyed, naïve dreamer, nor constantly high-fiving and air-punching. This is a practical passion for business, for how business works, for what business is.

Importantly, while you need to be interested in what you do, you do not need to be passionate about the product. Passion for your product or service can fade – it can wilt, and burn out like the early passion of a new love affair. Passion for business is different. It's passion for the challenge, passion for the activity, passion for the money you are making.

An example who springs to mind is Garry Nicholls, the man I mentioned earlier who created an online business selling clotheslines. Is he passionate about clotheslines? Not really. Is he passionate about business? You bet he is. He loves his customers – he loves finding new ways to connect with them, and to create repeat business. He ended up selling this business to a bigger player in the clothesline world and is busy building his next business.

10. CAN YOU HANDLE ROUTINE?

Sometimes, it can all feel like Groundhog Day. There are repetitive processes to be followed, routine activities that keep the business functioning and tedious tasks to do. I remember meeting a woman who had started a yoga business and, after five years, never wanted to see another yoga mat, downward dog or sun salutation. Her beloved yoga had become routine. Being able to continue with what needs to be done, and commit to the activities that are the backbone of your business success, is important. There are also solutions – perhaps this woman needed to hire other instructors and do less of the technical side of things herself. As we'll discuss later, it *is* possible to outsource some of the tedium, but there will always be an element of routine, so you have to be comfortable with that.

11. ARE YOU THE SORT OF PERSON WHO CAN CREATE STANDARD PROCESSES AND PROCEDURES?

Okay, I can virtually see your eyes rolling ... I have heard pretty much every objection there is about standardising the way you do what you do. But the real secret to business success is having standard operating procedures – having consistent ways to achieve the same outcome.

One of my favourite clients, now a really good friend, is a 'Master of Process'. I vividly remember us sitting in her small office in Sydney. It used to be the boardroom of an architecture firm and was above a toy shop on a busy road on the way to Sydney airport. I think I worked about three hours a fortnight helping with the financials. Another person worked a couple of half days doing orders and someone else helped with scheduling a few hours a month. My friend – we'll call her Rachel – did pretty much everything else. One day, Rachel began writing up a policy and procedures manual, and someone asked, 'Why do we need a policy and procedures manual? It's just us!' She replied, 'It won't always be "just us".'

She was right. Today, Rachel's business employs ten people and turns over multiple millions in revenue, and a significant part of the success can be attributed to having solid policies and procedures. When someone goes on holidays or has a sick day, anyone can do their job. Last year, Rachel took six weeks off to travel in South America and the business continued successfully, with her only checking in from time to time when Internet connection permitted. This is the power of systems and processes. Think of them as the asset they are and not some burden to be endured.

12. DO YOU LOVE TO LEARN NEW THINGS?

By the time your business is operating, the world will already be different. It is imperative that, as a business owner, you are constantly seeking to learn and innovate. You'll need to find new and different ways to surprise and delight your customers. What is special today may be standard by next month. I can remember the first time I used a fax machine. We were all in awe of the technology. Now no one even uses fax machines – and I'm not even that old! When Skype first launched, we were all amazed at the idea that we could call someone across the world and *see* them, pretty much for free, the only cost being the actual data. Skype was, and remains, a free service. Now there are many ways to talk face to face with people anywhere in the world; there's Facebook Messenger, Whatsapp ... And who knows what else is coming?

13. ARE YOU COMPETITIVE?

'You bet I am,' is the correct response here. Do you realise it is a competition? Other people in your industry are called competitors for a reason. Every minute of every day, your customers and clients are deciding how they will spend their limited resources, whether that is money, time or energy. They have a choice between spending with you or with another business. You need to be competitive enough to care which choice they make!

14. CAN YOU FOCUS ON ONE THING?

We are constantly told that women are good at multi-tasking, and, in general, as workers, everyone needs to be able to multi-task. However, the evidence shows that the greatest success comes from being able to focus. I often use a timer. I set the timer for fifteen minutes and do just one thing till the timer goes off. Sometimes, I make it twenty-five minutes, forty-five minutes or even just five minutes. It is a great way to create laser focus on a particular task.

The level of addiction to checking phones, Instagram, Facebook, SnapChat, Twitter and the like is being described as the equivalent of a drug or alcohol addiction. The same dopamine trigger takes place when we see someone has responded to a post or message, and people have become addicted to the dopamine hit.

One of the key ways to stand out in the future will be the ability to stay focused and contain that desire to constantly check social. Turn it off when you're working and focus on the business tasks at hand.

15. ARE YOU ABLE TO ADAPT QUICKLY TO CHANGING CIRCUMSTANCES?

Or are you the sort of person who likes regularity and certainty? Being in business can be tumultuous, ambiguous and uncertain; cash flow can be erratic, clients demanding, suppliers' timing might fluctuate, and predicting the right product mix can be a gamble.

I believe that, for many people, creating your own business can still give you a level of certainty that is missing from many companies and organisations where people work. However, you have to be able to adapt to changing circumstances. You have to stay on your toes and manage whatever comes up.

Activity: Personal Fit

Get out your notebook and answer the fifteen questions. Before you move on, make sure you've answered every single one in detail. Think of examples where you've shown you'll be able to apply yourself to your new business. Do you have what it takes?

You can download the above Do You Have What it Takes? questions on a worksheet at http://www.healthynumbers.com.au/ book-templates/

If you have answered 'yes' to most of the questions in this chapter, then creating your own business – with the right idea – might just be for you. But there are other questions to ask in terms of having what it takes. Now that we've seen if you are the right personality fit, we need to look at the financial fit.

ARE YOUR PERSONAL FINANCES IN ORDER?

I was heading into the city for a client meeting and happened to bump into Gayle at the train station. I hadn't seen her for a while and asked how she was going. 'I've been offered a full-time job,' she told me. 'That's where I'm going now.' Gayle and I had met about a year earlier at one of our local networking events. She was a copy writer with her own business, so I was curious why she had accepted a full-time job. 'I ran out of money,' she explained. 'I need the job for cash flow. I'm still working on growing my business at the weekends.'

Gayle is not alone in needing to return to paid employment to supplement her business startup. I can think of several others. There's Jackie, who had a fabulous idea for specialty wine education. She ended up taking a full-time marketing job when her money ran out, and now holds her specialty classes on weekends and evenings. There's Kate, who had a fabulous business – importing novelty handbags and purses and selling them at the market. She found a full-time job as a business development manager for a handbag manufacturer, and this actually enables her to enjoy the best of both worlds – her love of handbags and her passion for selling – while also enjoying a steady income.

Over the past ten years, I have met many people with great ideas for creating their own businesses who have taken the leap only to find they run out of money before the business really gets going. This is most often when they seek help and find me.

Getting your personal finances in order before you start your business is critical. There are five steps you can take:

1. Get really clear about how much you need to live – every day, every week, every month.

2. Get real about your debt: credit cards, short-term loans, student loans, any other amounts owing. What is the total outstanding debt and how much do you have to pay each month to pay back your debt? Each week?

3. Add your debt repayment amounts to your annual expenses. This total amount is called your 'Buffer Balance'.

4. Open a separate bank account in your name and refer to it as your 'Business Buffer Account'.

5. Most financial experts will suggest you need to have the amount of your total annual expenses – your buffer balance – saved and sitting in this separate bank account. I would agree. So start saving!

A couple of years ago, I was fortunate enough to meet Jane Wurwand, the woman who founded Dermalogica with her husband in 1983. She was speaking at a conference I attended and I found her personal story inspiring. One of the things I remember her saying was that for the first five years, they didn't have the time or the money to go clothes or shoe shopping because, at first, they didn't have any spare time. Every minute of every waking hour was spent building and growing their business. And every penny they had was being invested in the business.

Of course, being at a conference made up almost entirely of women, the 'no shoe shopping for five years' comment raised a laugh from most of the audience. However, her point was an important one. They didn't eat out during those five years because every penny was going into the business. Her message was clear – if you are serious about being in business then you just might need to make financial sacrifices in order to be successful.

Dermalogica remains a privately owned company today. This means they are not owned by a beauty conglomerate, holding company or financiers. They take pride in being true pioneers in their industry and they are driven by education and research. Launching the school that became the first International Dermal Institute (IDI) in Marina Del Rey in 1983, they went on two years later to start developing products that were free of the common irritants and could be used for sensitive and problem skin. The business is now based in 145,000-square-foot corporate headquarters in Los Angeles, and the products are sold in more than eighty countries. There are more than 100,000 trained skin therapists around the globe. A pretty inspiring case study.

So let's take a closer look at the process you can take to get your finances in order.

1. GET REALLY CLEAR ABOUT HOW MUCH IT COSTS YOU TO LIVE

Track your spending for a whole month – every ... single ... cent. This will give you a good idea of how much money you need to live. Each and every client that I have ever worked with who has completed this has been astounded at where their money goes and where they spend the most money. I remember, years ago, a client saying to me, 'You know, Ingrid, it's not the Italian shoes and silk blouses that blow my budget; it's the magazines, chocolate bars and coffees.'

At the same time, get out all your bills and bank statements and credit card statements, and identify all of your annual expenses. How much have you spent on each item over the past twelve months?

While these expenses will be different for each person, there are some basics across a few common categories. Here is a starting list, but you can add additional categories, or change them around:

Housing

- Rent
- Mortgage
- Electricity

- Gas
- Water
- Rates
- Insurance
- Telephone
- Internet
- Repairs and maintenance
- Cleaner; gardener

Transport

- Petrol
- Road Tolls
- Registration
- Insurance
- Weekly/monthly travel ticket
- Maintenance
- Storage, parking

Basic Living

- Food – groceries
- Food – coffees, eating out
- Cleaning items

Exercise

- Gym membership
- Yoga
- Personal trainer
- Sport

Personal Care

- Medical insurance
- Doctors
- Dentist
- Specialists
- Prescriptions/medication
- 'Lotions and potions'
- Make-up
- Nails
- Hairdresser
- Massage

Pets and Related Costs

- Vet expenses
- Food
- Vaccinations
- Flea treatment
- Beauty parlour

Child Expenses

- Food
- Clothing and shoes
- Childcare
- Education
- Books, uniforms, etc.
- Sporting equipment and sporting lessons
- Gadgets and toys
- Medical and medicine

- Dental
- Tuck shop
- Pocket money
- Gifts for other children

Other Living

- Socialising – dinner with friends, drinks nights
- Memberships – sport, clubs, interest groups
- Subscriptions – online, magazines
- Clothes and shoes – yours and other family members'
- Gifts, presents, cards – for birthdays, family, Christmas, weddings, babies
- Entertainment – theatre, concerts, Stan, Foxtel, sporting events
- Holidays – travel, weekends, day trips
- Books – physical books and magazines, e-books, Kindle, gadgets
- Stationery

When you look at your monthly spending tracker and your overall analysis of your annual costs, this will allow you to calculate how much money you need to live for a year, which you can break down per month and week. It may also help you realise where you could reduce spending.

2. GET REAL ABOUT YOUR DEBT

What is the total of your outstanding debt and how much do you have to pay each month or week?

How quickly can you get your debts paid down? When you reduce debt, you improve your cash flow. When you reduce credit card debt, you reduce the amount of interest you are paying. I had a client who paid so much interest in one year on her credit card that it would have paid for a first class airfare to New York and a two-week holiday. It really is a no-brainer to stop paying credit card interest.

Make it a priority to pay down any outstanding debts, especially where interest rates are high.

3. ADD YOUR CALCULATED DEBT REPAYMENT AMOUNTS TO YOUR CALCULATED ANNUAL EXPENSES

This total amount is called your Buffer Balance, mentioned earlier in this chapter, and tells you the total amount of money that you spend in a twelve-month period. You need to know this because if your business makes no money for the first year, you need to know that you can afford to live for the first twelve months while you are building your business income. This Buffer Balance allows you to eat and have somewhere to sleep.

The truth is that many businesses make little or no money in the first year, and even into the second and third years as well. One of the most debilitating aspects of being in business is worrying where your income will come from. I have met many business people who do not sleep at night because they are worried about how they are going to pay their bills. It is even more difficult to run a business when you are sleep-deprived.

If your business does start to generate enough income to make a profit in your early years, you will most likely be spending that money on additional services to grow your business rather than paying yourself a large salary. I recently met an entrepreneur who paid himself and his wife a total of $5,000 a year for the first two years they were in business. All other funds were channelled back into growing their business.

There is a school of thought that says that a business startup will be more motivated to generate business and income if they have no money to fall back on. I'm not sure I agree with this. It certainly wouldn't be true for me. I feel a sense of calm when I have enough money and that sense of calm allows me to be my best self and create great products and services for my clients. If I were worried about paying my rent and feeding myself and my cats, I wouldn't be able to do what I need to do for my clients. What do you think? Do you believe you might be more motivated by the *need* to make money in your business? It makes more sense to have a comfortable buffer – this enables you get started and not find yourself in the position where you have to take a job and restrict your business building to the weekends.

4. OPEN A BUSINESS BUFFER ACCOUNT

Most financial experts will suggest you need to have one year's expenses saved and sitting in a separate bank account before you start your business and I would agree. Your Buffer Balance is the amount I would suggest saving and stashing in this separate account.

I firmly believe that this needs to be a completely separate account, only to be accessed if and when necessary. If the account requires an extra password or has some other deterrent from taking out the funds, that can be beneficial as it can help you think twice about spending that money.

There are a number of banking institutions that offer high-interest bank accounts for relatively low fees. For people who have a mortgage on their home, another way to sanction these funds would be to hold them in a mortgage off-set account. It's always best to check with your accountant or financial advisor which would be best alternative for your individual situation.

5. START SAVING NOW

Several people have said to me that it's impossible to save that much money, and I can understand that, for some people, it may *seem* impossible, but here are my thoughts on the matter.

There are a few different solutions for people who want to start right away and save as they go along, and I would usually suggest some combination of the following, depending on the individual situation:

Working part-time: Take a part-time job that pays enough to survive on and then use the non-work days to create and build your business. There are many people who choose this path and it can be a viable solution.

Continuing to work full-time: Create and build your business on the weekends and in the evenings. There are people who have managed to make this work for them really well. In fact, some people really like their career and want to earn a bit extra on the side by creating a business.

Negotiating extended leave from work: Some organisations offer half-paid annual leave or long service leave. This can be a solid block of concentrated time to create and build your business in three months or six months while receiving constant income. I have seen some people do this quite successfully. Having the time constraint can, in some cases, create greater incentive to focus.

Reducing spending on the non-essentials: Take a good, hard look at the items and expenses on the lists you created and think about where could these be reduced. This would enable you to save more money and save more quickly. I have seen people realise just how much money they spend on what are really non-essential items; when they cut them out altogether, they manage to pay down debt quickly and start saving.

Some people don't want to go through a transition phase, however, and if they're the same ones who think saving in advance of starting their business is impossible, they need to face a hard truth. Where someone lacks fiscal discipline – the ability to manage your own money, and further, lacks the wherewithal, desire, drive or ambition to actually *take control of their personal finances* and save any amount of Buffer Balance before starting a business, then I seriously question if they truly have what it takes to run a successful business. The reality, for some people, is that they would be better off reconsidering the idea of creating their own business and stay forever in their job.

If someone is unable to create financial discipline in their personal life then I would seriously question their ability to create and run a fiscally responsible and successful business.

The stronger your desire to get started, the more imaginative you will be about how to get your personal finances in order. One of my clients cleared out their cupboards and shed, sold things on eBay, and held a huge garage sale to raise extra money to fund her business startup. The more passionate you are about minimising expenses so you can save more, the more diligent you will be about reducing credit card debt and avoiding unnecessary items.

As a very good friend of mine said some years ago: 'Do for five years what no one else will do and you can do for the rest of your life what no one else will be able to do.' This echoes finance guru Dave Ramsey, who said, 'If you live like no one else, later you can live like no one else.'

Ask yourself: how much do you really want to build your own business? It's time to get your personal finances in order.

Activity: Financial Fit

Go through each of the five steps above, and thoroughly address your finances. Ask the hard questions – how much do you really spend and what could you save if you got creative about it? Record your plan to amass your Buffer Balance.

DO YOU HAVE A BUSINESS MINDSET?

We've looked at the pros and cons of creating your own business. The reason many people give for starting their own business is their desire to be their own boss. Many also want that sense of achievement that goes with creating something from the ground up. Of course, these are admirable reasons and I can totally relate to both. However, for a business to be a business, it does need to make money – a profit. A business that is not making money is actually a hobby. So a great question to ask right now is: am I starting a business or is it more of a hobby?

When does one become the other? For many people thinking about getting started in business, it comes from doing something they really enjoy doing: being a florist or a photographer, making cupcakes, doing Pilates or yoga, having acupuncture, concentrating on their nutrition, or any of a whole other host of things. What can result is a sideline business, where you stay in your corporate job and form your startup in your spare time. At some stage, it might become apparent that the business is actually generating enough money that you could work part-time and run the business part-time.

Generally, you would be considered to be in business for tax purposes if you enter into an activity with the intention of running it as a profit-making business, and if the activity is carried out in a way that shows it has a significant commercial purpose and viability.

So what does this mean? In essence:

- Intention of running it as a profit-making business means making money so that you can pay yourself and have money remaining to reinvest in your business.

- Significant commercial purpose and viability means paying yourself enough money so that you might be able to eventually make your business your full-time income and/or employ others to run the business.

Developing a business mindset is part of the journey of getting started. It's a way of thinking about the business *as a business*. A person with a business mindset understands what it means to be in business and approaches their startup with the delicious anticipation and total expectation that their business will generate income and they will maximise profit; the business will make money for them and their shareholders, partners, clients and team members. And this is a good thing.

Many of my clients say to me, 'Ingrid, it's not just about the money', and, of course, this can be true. However, if there is no money, there is no business. When there is no money, there is no way to buy the things you need, like an Internet connection and equipment. There is no money to pay suppliers, or to pay rent and so on. When there is no money, you don't sleep at night.

Many of the people I have worked with over the years want to help people, and this is a noble desire. I'm in business to help people as well, so I fully understand. However, if you are not making enough money to pay your expenses and have sufficient to pay yourself a good wage, then how can you help anyone? It's hard to help anyone if you are sleeping in a car under the bridge.

Having a business mindset also means knowing how much everything costs, and I'm not just talking about the physical items you purchase with real money – it includes knowing the cost of your time and your efforts.

A few years ago, I was invited to a breakfast networking meeting where I sat beside a lawyer – let's call him Lawrence. He was telling me all about how successful his legal practice was. I asked him how he got most of his clients and whether he got many from this particular networking group. 'Oh no, not really any from this group,' he said, 'mostly from word-of-mouth referrals from my existing clients.' I asked why he continued to attend the breakfast group and he said, 'It doesn't really cost much and they are nice enough people.'

'How much does it cost you?' I asked. Lawrence said, 'Breakfast is just $35.'

Now, I couldn't help thinking, 'He doesn't *really know* how much this breakfast costs him.'

Let's presume he attends forty-five of a potential fifty-two weekly meetings. This allows for holidays, out-of-town business trips or other reasons he might not attend.

Total cost of breakfast = $35 per meeting x 45 meetings = $1,575.00

It turns out there is also an annual membership fee = $1,150.00

Lawrence drives and parks his car = $3.30/hour x 2 hours = $6.60/ meeting x 45 weeks = $297.00

Vehicle expense: 7.5km x 2 = 15km per week x $0.74/km* = $11.10 x 45 weeks = $499.50

Unbillable time: 2 hours (at least) per week @ $500/hour = $1,000 per week x 45 weeks = $45,000

* In Australia, at the time of printing, the allowance for a kilometre of travel is $0.74/km

In total, if he attends the breakfast meeting for forty-five weeks of the year, his cost is $1,575 + $1,150 + $297 + $499.50 + $45,000.00 = $48,521.50

The table on the next page illustrates Lawrence's spending and the costs associated with networking events in more detail.

Cost involved	Calculation	Cost to Lawrence
Total cost of breakfast he attends	$35 per meeting x 45 meetings	$ 1 575.00
"Make-up" breakfasts he does not attend	$35 x 7 "Make-ups" (52–45 = 7)	$ 245.00
Annual membership	Per year of membership	$ 1 150.00
Parking cost for each meeting	Parking $3.30 x 2 hours x 45 meetings	$ 297.00
Vehicle expense	7.5 km x 2 (return trip) X $0.74/km x 45 meetings	$ 499.50
Billable time	2 hours (at least) per week x $500/ hour x 45 weeks	$45 000.00
Total Cost of attending networking breakfast		$ 48 766.50

The reality is that Lawrence often stays after the meeting and chats. He also arranges individual coffee meetings with others there. Networking is, of course, a critical aspect of any business and if meeting people one-to-one is a really important part of your business model, then a breakfast networking group like this may well be worth the financial cost.

Lawrence also enjoys the company of the group, but the question for him to ask himself with his business-mindset hat on is: 'Is there $48,500+ worth of value in attending every week of the year?' If the answer is 'yes', then it is a great investment of his time and his financial resources. If the answer is 'no', then it might be time to look for a different networking group.

In contrast to Lawrence, an accountant friend of mine attends a similar meeting and the lead generation from the people he meets more than ten times pays the cost of attending. It takes a business mindset to make these calculations and figure out the true cost of activities, whether it is networking, training, or creating and building relationships with new clients.

Activity: Business Mindset

It's time for you to get out your notebook again. This time, you're going to calculate the true cost of an activity in a similar way to the breakdown I've done for Lawrence's breakfast networking.

Think about some activity you do on a regular basis. Maybe coffee with a colleague or a departmental meeting.

Calculate the costs involved. Consider all of the costs, just as in Lawrence's example. Then truly consider the value of the benefits. Remember, some of the benefits might be intangible.

It's a good habit to get into to be able to complete a calculation such as this because over the time you are in business, you will be faced with decisions that require a cost/benefit analysis. This is exactly what you've just done by completing this activity, and it wasn't that difficult, was it?

Making sure that your business is going to make money isn't about being greedy – it's about having a business mindset. This is one of the biggest factors when it comes to being successful. If you've decided you've got what it takes and have taken up the challenge to organise your finances, it's time to turn to the next element. It's time to test your idea.

2. YOUR IDEA

*'Noise proves nothing. Often a hen who
has merely laid an egg cackles as if she
has laid an asteroid.'*

MARK TWAIN

Years ago, I read a fable that went something like this ... The management of a shoe factory sent two marketing scouts out to a remote region of Africa to study the prospects for expanding their shoe business. The first marketing scout sent back a telegram saying: SITUATION HOPELESS STOP NO ONE WEARS SHOES. The second marketing scout sent back his telegram saying: GLORIOUS BUSINESS OPPORTUNITY STOP THEY HAVE NO SHOES.

Of course, today, there wouldn't be many parts of the world left for a shoe business to go looking for new opportunities, and we certainly wouldn't be using telegrams to communicate. But I really like this as an example of how different people can be. Where one person sees a 'hopeless situation', the other sees a 'glorious business opportunity'. This fable still rings true today, and never more so than when we consider people's different ideas for starting a business.

The secret to business success is being able to recognise where there is an opportunity to offer to the market something that:

- Provides a valuable solution to a need people have (through a product or service).

- People are prepared to pay you money for.

Being a success in business is really as simple as this.

Another thing I really love about the fable above is that it is a classic example of a situation where customers do not even know they're missing what is being offered. The people in the fable don't need shoes, but as a very good friend of mine likes to remind me, 'People rarely buy what they need; they buy what they want.'

This is one of the really tricky things about being in business. Your great idea is just that – *your* great idea, and right now, the reality is that your potential customers may not even know they need or want what you are going to offer.

Being a successful business is all about helping your potential clients understand that what you offer is something they value enough to reach into their pockets, take out their wallets and pay you money.

In this chapter, we look at the following when it comes to your business idea: what does your business really offer – what is it really selling? And why will people buy it? Going through these questions will lead you to the ultimate realisation: whether or not your business idea is viable.

CHOOSING ONE MAIN IDEA TO WORK ON

I was talking with a client, Kate, and she told me that she has so many ideas that she doesn't have time to implement them all. I know how that feels. Like Kate and many others, you may be buzzing with so many ideas for creating a new business that you really don't know where to start.

Over the past ten years, I've been working with people planning their business startups, and over and over, they say that one of the key benefits of having a business of their own will be the opportunity to be creative. This can be especially appealing to people who feel their creativity is currently stifled or constrained in some way. And it's true! Being able to have creative expression is certainly a great benefit of being in your own business. However, in this planning stage, it is a good idea to try to find one main idea to work on and stick to it.

So how do you know which one main idea to work with? How do you choose where to start? If only we had a crystal ball. We could see into the future and check which ideas will work out and to what extent. If only. The reality is, there are so many influencing factors, and many are completely beyond our control. So we have to focus on those under our direct influence.

I'll give you a clue – choosing the big idea is tied up with the definition of passion and having passion for your business. I mentioned earlier that you don't necessarily need to be super passionate about the product – remember Gary Nicholls? Gary set up a business selling clotheslines. Were clotheslines his passion? Not really. While you don't necessarily need to be passionate about your product, you do need to be passionate about being in business. My definition of passion is energy.

Right now, you may have quite a few great ideas swirling around. Maybe you've written a few in a journal or on a few sticky notes on your computer or bathroom mirror. Which idea out of the list do you have the most passion – the most energy – for?

Activity: Great Ideas

Take a new page in your notebook and title it: 'Great ideas'.

List out as many ideas as you can think of.

Now look at the list and consider:

1. Which ones do you really feel passionate about?

2. Which ones might be easiest to produce a basic product for?

3. Which ones might it be easiest to make some money on?

Use the rankings that arise out of these questions to choose your one main idea to focus on.

This next section looks at ways of assessing this great idea.

DO YOU SOLVE A REAL PROBLEM WITH YOUR BUSINESS IDEA?

People do not buy products; they buy solutions to their problems. The problem always comes first and the product or service always comes second.

So, right now, you've got your great idea. The key thing for you to figure out is what problem it solves.

Let me be really clear here, there are almost no products or services that are purely about *creating joy, pleasure or beauty*. When we drill down, almost every single one of them can be identified as *solving the problem of sadness, pain or ugliness* (respectively).

First, let's look at an example of an obvious and tangible problem seeking a solution. It's worth noting that every problem has multiple solutions and, in fact, every solution potentially solves multiple problems.

Problem = I'm hungry

Possible solutions = buy food or drink, or stay hungry

Of course, this then leads to a myriad of choices under 'buy food'. I can buy ingredients and make something. I can buy something quick or tasty or healthy or expensive. The possibilities are endless.

I was at a startup Meetup a couple of years ago and one of the speakers was Steve Baxter. At the time, he had just set up his Tech StartUp Lab in Brisbane Riverside Labs (this is the same Steve who is one of the Sharks on Australia's version of *Shark Tank*).

Steve told a story about a man who had created a product specifically to save the unused piece of a cucumber when someone makes a salad. This man had spent a lot of time and energy inventing this small device that stored the unused portion of cucumber. His idea was to save it from going soft and keep it fresh for future use. The inventor had developed a prototype and made modifications to the point where he could keep cucumbers fresh for almost seven days after they had first been cut for use. It's a true story – seven days!

The inventor was about to mortgage his house in order to have thousands of these cucumber savers made for world distribution. He was commissioning a company to create his online store when he met Steve Baxter, just by chance, and told him all about his plans.

'Does anyone want your cucumber saver?' Steve asked.

'Everyone will want one,' the inventor replied.

'That may well be the case. But do you *know* they want one? What evidence do you have that they want one?'

This is the critical question: what evidence do you have?

Solving problems is at the core of every business. Solving problems for people who will pay for your solution is what will make your business a success. You may be in love with your great idea, but the test is this: is anyone else enough in love with your idea to want to pay you their hard-earned money for it?

So it is not enough just to think about the problem you solve. Your great idea needs to solve a problem for people who:

- Know they have a problem (interestingly, your potential clients might need assistance to recognise they have a problem that needs your solution – like the Africans would in the fable).

- Realise that your solution is the answer to their problem (here, they'll definitely need to know why they should pick your solution rather than anyone else's).

- Are prepared to pay your price for your solution.

The movie *Joy* demonstrates all three of these points. Joy Mangano's potential customers hadn't realised there was a problem with their existing mops. She showed them their problem and then solved it for them with her miracle mop. She then offered it at a price they could afford.

How will you know if your idea does this? Research. Testing. Asking your potential clients. This is all part of your planning. Getting this right is one of the critical aspects of business. You don't want to be the next cucumber saver man. The next section covers how best to go about this using the concept of the Minimum Viable Product or MVP.

IS YOUR IDEA SIMPLE TO DEVELOP?

Some business ideas will be easier than others to 'take to market'. If you are a photographer working in a company taking photos every day and you decide that you want to start your own photography business, you already have the skills, knowledge and expertise to take photos. If you are a chef working in a restaurant and you have an idea for your own restaurant or café, you too have the skills, knowledge and expertise to do all the activities necessary to run the food side of the restaurant or café. If you are building a business based on what you already know and what you already do, then you may find it relatively simple to create your product or service offering.

Alyce Tran was working as a (young) lawyer and looking for a stylish compendium for her papers. She couldn't find one at the price and quality she was looking for so she designed her own. This was mid–2014. She and her business partner Yanya Liu launched a small collection in three colours which sold out in three days via Instagram. Her company TDE now offers multiple products and at the time of printing reports sales of $15 million. Alyce and Tanys didn't start with a full range of products, however. They created a Minimum Viable Product (MVP) as their first offer to the market.

The concept of Minimum Viable Product comes from the Lean Startup methodology by Eric Ries (2011). The methodology aims to shorten product development cycles. Lean manufacturing has its beginnings in efforts to streamline production processes as far back as 1906 with Henry Ford. It developed further in the 1950s in Japan and in the 1990s was embodied by Motorola's Six Sigma tools for process improvement. The Lean Startup methodology asserts that 'lean has nothing to do with how much money a company raises'; rather, it has everything to do with assessing the specific demands of consumers and how to meet that demand using the least amount of resources possible. The MVP is generally used to assist tech startups and refers to developing your product with only the core features needed for it to be deployed into the potential market. Basically, using an MVP means you don't have to launch your full offering with all the bells and whistles – you probably need less to start off than you think you do. An MVP is a product, or service, with just enough features so that it represents the product for research purposes. If we take Alyce Tran's compendium example, it was a fully representative compendium in only three basic colours.

This is a form of beta testing. You take an MVP to market to ensure that there is, in fact, market demand. One of the key premises of Lean Startup is the continual learning loop. I believe this can be applied to any idea for any new business. Think back to the man inventing the device to save cucumbers. If he had gone to market with a basic prototype and asked if anyone wanted his product, he might have saved a lot of time and energy. He may well have developed something even better and more useful. Developing an MVP avoids creating or building products that no one wants and saves wasted resources and energy.

Every business needs to create a beta model of their offering, take it to their potential customers and get feedback early and often. Use the feedback to make changes and to modify the product or service. Then take that back to market, ask again, and test and learn. It is a continuous process.

Let's take our photographer, for example. Kevin works for a photography studio and decides he wants to create his own studio specialising in taking photos of pets, specifically cats. He creates a basic product: *I take photos of your cat and this is what you get*, and heads to the marketplace to test if there is demand. Based on the feedback he receives, he is then able to modify his product.

I believe Facebook is a great real-world example of this process. Mark Zuckerberg knew he wanted to create an online social community and he started with college students, taking the learnings to modify the initial product.

Testing an MVP will particularly help people who want to start a business in an area they haven't worked in before. I have one client who wants to start a flower shop. What she is doing currently is about as far from selling flowers as you can get. So she is testing the demand for her niche flowers by taking a stand at a local weekend market so that she can talk to and listen to her potential clients and learn more specifically what will work for her business.

If we look at my business, when I started work on the online course 'So You Want to Start a Business', I took my MVP to a classroom and tested the modules on students face to face. I took their feedback and made changes, and that formed the basis of my online training program that now has students not only across Australia but around the world.

MVP gives you a way to test what the market needs and is willing to pay, before you invest huge amounts of your money, time and energy. Nathan Furr and Paul Ahlstrom, co-authors of the book *Nail It, Then Scale It*, 2015, said it best: 'Which would you rather do? Talk to customers now and find out you were wrong or talk to customers a year and thousands of dollars down the road and still find out you were wrong?'

Activity: Your MVP

Consider how you can create a beta or basic version of your idea – an MVP – so that you can take it to your potential market and test it out.

Think about Alyce and Tanya and their compendium. What is the minimum you could create to take to market?

A key point to understand regarding the concept of 'minimum' as it applies to MVP is that the quality of the product or service is still as high as you can make it. It is not a sub-standard version of your offering. Minimum in this context means the easiest-to-produce, least complex demonstration of your product.

So you have your MVP ready to take to market. Now you want to find out whether your business idea will make a profit. How do you know if it is financially viable?

The key questions to answer at this point are:

- Does anybody want to buy what you're selling?

- Are they prepared to pay money for what you're selling?

- Are they prepared to pay enough money for the business to be financially viable?

For example, your idea is to source and sell candles at the market. You buy the candles for $10 each. When you go to the market, people only want to pay $5 for each candle. Or maybe they'll pay you $10 for each candle. So far, this business model is not looking financially viable. You cannot sustain a business where the amount you are paid is less than the cost of buying or producing the product or service.

Large supermarkets have what they call 'loss leaders'. This is where they can afford to sell an item for less than they pay for it. This attracts customers to the supermarket and, as we all know, once they are in there, they'll buy more than they thought they were going to. This is the whole reason for the 'loss leader'. However, most small businesses cannot afford a loss-leader style financial model. If you're buying candles for $10, you need to know that you will be able to sell them for more than $10. And you need to do more than ask the question and trust that people are telling you the truth.

One of the interesting things about human behaviour and intention is that what we intend to do can be quite different to what we actually do.

When I met Peter Alexander, I was running P'leisure Wear by Ingrid Louise. We were discussing the pros and cons of manufacture in Australia versus manufacturing in China. He told me that he had asked his customers if, given the choice, they would choose Australian-made pyjamas rather than Chinese-made pyjamas. Even if the price was a little bit more. And his customers told him that they would choose Australian-made pyjamas. This was the customers' 'intention'. However, the reality was that, given the choice when they came to actually make their purchase, people chose the cheaper Chinese-made pyjamas. And this had a large impact on his business model at the time.

An important lesson for us from these examples is that, in order to establish the financial viability of our business, we need to know that people will *actually* pay, not just what they have an intention to pay. The way we distinguish between intention and actual purchasing behaviour is to physically take our products or services to the market and find our customers.

Let's look at the example of the candle. If we ask people, 'Would you pay $15 for this candle?' they might say, 'Yes.' This would not be sufficient research to start your candle business. To truly test the price point, people need to actually reach into their wallets, take out the cash and hand you the $15 in exchange for the candle.

That's the evidence we spoke about earlier. And it's important because the financial commitment can go much further than buying the candles to sell. I had a client in one of my workshops who made candles and her dream was to open candle shop. One of the things we spoke about was the financial commitment involved in signing up for a commercial lease. It is a huge financial risk to take a commercial lease for a shop if you're not 1,000 per cent sure – yes 1,000 per cent sure, not just 100 per cent certain – that there is a market for the product that you're selling, whether it's candles or clothes or shoes or food.

Some ways of testing the candle market might be:

- Having a stall at local street fairs held by schools or churches.

- Having a stall at local craft markets held at weekends.

- Approaching department stores.

- Approaching other shops that sell products that your ideal customer might also be buying. (We're going to look at the concept of the ideal customer in great detail in the next chapter.) For example, you might approach dress shops or jewellery stores, and put the candles into the shop on consignment.

- Having a stand at a conference your ideal clients attend.

There is an expression: 'Build the plane as you fly it'. What this means is that, sometimes, we can presell our product or service before we actually finish developing it. For example, the candle lady might visit stores with a sample, and then, when she has an order for 100 candles, she commits to making them, rather than making 100 candles of a particular size and colour and trying to sell them.

Another example is a project I was involved in for a Federal Government department. There was a tender calling for expressions of interest regarding running a one-day program across Australia. The company that won the tender put together the proposal knowing they would need to recruit a certain number of facilitators and trainers and that they would also need to put together the actual one-day program. It was only when they actually won the tender that they went into the detail of recruitment and instructional design.

Activity: Testing Viability

Think about your business idea. Make a list of places where can you start testing the market to see if there are people willing to pay the price, as in the candle example above.

Actually ask people to buy your MVP or pre-order your products or services. This is how you will decide whether your idea is financially viable.

One of my clients makes beautiful scarves (http://www. sophierobertson.com) and when she first started her business, she took examples of her scarves into her workplace. They sold like hotcakes! This helped her understand which scarves her market wanted and were prepared to pay for.

In the next section, we're going to look who else has the same idea. Who is your competition and how can they help you?

IS YOUR IDEA BETTER THAN THE REST?

I live about a ten-minute walk from my nearest suburban train station along a busy main road in an inner-city suburb of Sydney. A few months ago, I wanted to have my hair washed and dried because I was going to an event and wanted that look that only going to the hairdresser can achieve. I thought, 'I'll drop into one of the hairdressers on the way home and see if I can book an appointment. One of them is bound to have an available appointment on a Wednesday afternoon.'

If you had asked me how many hairdressers there are on this particular stretch of road, I would have said, 'Maybe six.' How many are there? There are nineteen hairdressing salons and four barbershops in the six blocks between the train station and the road I live on! Isn't it interesting what we notice and what we don't? I knew we had a few hairdressers in the area. I wouldn't have said a total of twenty-three hair-related businesses. That's a lot of competition.

When you are thinking about your business idea, there are two ways to look at your competition:

- Direct competition

- Indirect competition.

Direct competition is made up of the businesses that offer the same products or services that you do. In my example, each of the nineteen hairdressers offered pretty much the same thing in that they could all wash, cut, colour and dry hair.

Indirect competition is made up of all the other products and services that are on offer to satisfy a need or want of the customer. So in my hairdresser example, washing my hair at home would have been a form of indirect competition.

In another example, I've been working with a boutique wine producer. In the past, the wine industry thought their direct competition was other wine producers and their indirect competition was beer, spirits, cocktails and alcopops. In recent years, the wine industry has come to realise that their indirect competition is really any drink and not just other alcoholic drinks.

Many businesses find it relatively straightforward to identify the direct competition, but identifying the indirect competition is equally important. In fact, the more comprehensive your examination of the indirect competition, the more insight you will have into what is needed to make your business stand out in a crowded marketplace.

I believe that competition is a good thing. Being in an industry where there are others offering similar products or services is helpful when it comes to making your business a success. Trying to create a whole new business for something that has never been done before is incredibly hard work. Have you ever watched one of the very large aircraft trying to take off along the runway? Maybe you've been sitting in one and felt the amount of power it takes to lift that large aircraft off the ground. Starting any business is already like getting an A380 or a Boeing 747 off the ground. And trying to start a business doing something that has never been done before is even more difficult. If you have competition, you can analyse it.

I have another client who is thinking about starting a yoga school. She loves yoga, she has studied yoga for many years, and she dreams of running a yoga school and retreats which will make a difference in other people's lives.

She has identified her direct competition as other yoga schools, but her indirect competition is not so obvious. So far, she has identified:

- Pilates

- Gyms

- Private fitness training

- Running clubs

- Swimming

- Aqua aerobics

- Meditation centres

- Writing retreats

- Weight loss programs

- Bushwalking

- Rock climbing

- White water rafting

- Horse riding

- Sitting on the couch

- Going out for a glass of wine with a friend

And this list is not exhaustive. You may think of some that we haven't thought of yet, and she is certainly adding to her list. The point is to understand what else is out there in order to know your place in the scheme of things and make your idea more attractive than the alternatives.

Just recently, I met an art dealer who specialises in Australian Aboriginal art. He was telling me that people often say to him, 'Oh, you should take this art to New York.' He said to me, 'Why on earth would I do that? Why would I go somewhere they don't know who I am, they have never heard of me or my gallery, where most of the people know nothing about Australian Aboriginal art? Art is a luxury purchase that people make from someone they know, like and trust. It would most likely be years before anyone actually bought anything from me; the education and relationship building process would take years.'

How very insightful and wise. I can imagine there would be many people who, in the same situation, would jump at the chance to run to New York. And they might end up being successful, but then again, they might not. It's tough enough starting a business without venturing into a brand new environment. The key is to understand your business so you can analyse your competition and figure out how to achieve the best chance of success.

Working in a business where there are already successes helps your chances. How do you offer this same product or service in a way that is different, that is unique, that makes it yours?

Many years ago, I accepted a contract to work with a very successful family-run coffee roasting company. One of the owners, Paul, had always wanted to have his own café. He built a physically beautiful space and served the very best coffee and food. While he was gifted at sourcing and roasting coffee (at a time when small, boutique coffee roasters were a rarity in Sydney), he didn't really know much about staffing, managing and running a café. After a few years the family decided to sell the café and I was contracted to prepare it for sale.

While Paul didn't have a lot of experience in running cafés, he did have a solid understanding of business generally and how to serve his customers, and he made great coffee. One day, we were having a conversation about a new American coffee chain that was about to open its first store in Sydney. The industry was nervous. In the US, there is a Starbucks on every corner and our local newspapers were full of stories about 'the end of the local coffee shop'. This was just before the Sydney Olympics in 2000 and people were convinced that there was a coffee takeover on its way. There was genuine concern about what it would mean for the local industry. I remember asking Paul what he thought about Starbucks coming to Australia and he said, 'Competition is good because it keeps everyone on their toes. It is too easy for any business to become complacent and forget what really matters – customers matter, and our only reason for existing is to please and service our existing customers and the customers we don't yet have.'

What a terrific answer to my question. I felt it was a privilege to work with someone with such an attitude and approach. You have to foster this attitude in your own business and believe that competition is good because it keeps you on your toes – that's what can drive you to raise your idea above the rest!

It can also encourage you to niche.

'Niche' is a term that is used in ecological biology to define an organism's role in an ecosystem. Not only does a niche include the environment a given organism lives in, it also includes the organism's 'job' in that environment.

What is a niche in terms of business? Seth Godin talks about the 'Purple Cow' and standing out from the crowd. You may have heard of the black jellybean concept. This is the idea that while there are many colours of jellybeans, there are people who will just want the black ones.

Why is it considered important to find your niche? We are told it will contribute to your business success. As the experts say, you cannot be all things to all people. If you try, you end up not being attractive to any of them. Niching means focusing on one segment of the market, where you'll have less competition.

When I think about the nineteen hairdressers that exist in happy competition along the six blocks of road from my local train station to my home, one explanation for all their continued success is that they each have their own niche in the hairdressing market.

When I look at any street with a string of cafés all doing well, I believe the reason is because there are enough customers for all of them within each individual niche. To use the ecological definition above, they each have a job in their environment.

How do you feel about identifying a niche for your business? Let's take a look at the benefits:

- It allows you to build a strong presence in your market, as the expert in that particular area.

- It makes it easier to attract your ideal clients, the ones who want exactly what you offer.

- It helps you position your business and communicate what your brand stands for.

- It helps you maximise the money that you will spend on marketing because you know exactly where to focus your campaigns.

There's no rush to define your niche. It may end up being something that you define over time or it might be something you are very clear about from the beginning. It's up to you. Bear in mind, if you identify your niche early, it will affect your appraisal of your direct competition. If you don't identify it early, assessing your competition may direct you towards a gap in the market where you could niche.

Activity: Assess the Competition

Consider the following:

- What industry are you in? Do you have a niche?

- Who/what are your direct competitors?

- Who/what are your indirect competitors?

For each of these direct and indirect competitors, identify the following:

- What do they do that makes them successful?

- Why do customers choose their product/service?

Then consider these questions:

- What can you do to differentiate your business from others in the industry?

- What is not currently being offered in this industry? Is there a gap in the market where you could niche?

Once you've established whether your idea is really useful, whether it's financially viable and whom you're up against, you can look at whether you should consider any IP issues.

WHO OWNS THE IP?

IP stands for intellectual property. Depending on what sort of business you're considering starting, it could actually be a very valuable business asset, so it's important to understand what it is and how to protect it.

If you have an idea that will lead you to develop a new product or a new service, this is something that belongs to you. In order to own the IP, it needs to be registered. In Australia, you would register with IP Australia. Registering with IP Australia does not provide international protection, however. You need to apply separately for each country.

There are four basic types of IP protection:

PATENT

If you create a device, a method, a process or a substance that is new, innovative and useful, you can apply for a patent that will give you exclusive rights to that invention for a period of time. Patents can be legally enforced.

TRADEMARK

This is a symbol, letter, number, word, phrase, picture, logo or even a sound, smell or aspect of packaging that is used to distinguish the goods and services of one business from another business. It's important to remember that registering a business name is not the same as securing a trademark.

DESIGNS

Patents relate to function where design tends to relate to form. So design would feature shape configurations or patterns that give a product a unique appearance. The design must be distinctive and new in order to be registered.

COPYRIGHT

You can copyright works but not ideas. Copyright is most commonly applied to books, films, art, music and sound recordings. There are free and automatic legal rights given to the authors and creators of original works.

Sometimes, people believe that because they're small business, IP does not apply to them. But being small does not mean that you don't have legitimate IP that requires protection.

Here are some tips when it comes to protecting your idea:

- If you think you have an idea that is very new and innovative, it's best not to talk too much to too many people about that idea before you have explored the IP registration process.

- If you do need to discuss your idea with other people, it is important to have a legally binding non-disclosure agreement to protect your idea.

- Keep records and documentation of the development of your idea.

- If you engage contractors or employees in your business, it is important to include clauses in the contract regarding IP and confidentiality.

Here are a couple of examples to bear in mind. If you contract a photographer to take some photographs for you, it's important to know who owns the photographs at the end of the agreement. If you contract a designer to create a logo or book cover, it's important to know who owns these designs and have it established in a contract. It's easy to believe that you own them because they feel like yours, but you always need to check the fine print.

If you are currently working for someone else, check the contract of your employment. If you develop something while you're working for someone else, it's important to be clear about who owns that IP. If you're working on a side project while you have a job working for someone else, you might want to have a clause included that says anything you work on in your side project is yours to own. There is provision under Australian law that even if you are working on something as a side project in your holidays, the IP may still 'belong' to your employer. Best to check with the business's HR Manager or an independent HR specialist.

Activity: Protecting Your Idea

Consider whether you might need to register IP and obtain any patents or trademarks. Head to your country's relevant website to discover the detailed process you'll need to follow.

The best way to find the information for your country is to head to Google, type in the name of your country and 'register IP' or 'trademark' and that will list the agencies for your country.

Now we've looked at all these different aspects to consider when it comes to your idea, it's time to turn to the people your idea is for – your clients.

3. YOUR CLIENTS

'A lot of times people don't know what
they want until you show it to them.'

STEVE JOBS

Y ou may have heard the expression 'it takes two to tango'. If you have ever watched anyone dance the tango, you'll know that both partners are essential. They move in relation to one another. When we use this everyday expression, it commonly indicates that one person or entity is inextricably linked to another.

Your business is one of these tango dancers and your client is your dance partner. You are inextricably linked. The two critical aspects to a successful business are, in their simplest form:

- One party offers something for sale (a product or a service).
- One party buys that product or service.

It's as simple as that, really.

'They' – the second party – are out there. You just need to find them. The first step to finding them is to identify the key characteristics of your ideal client.

When you think about your main idea, whom do you imagine you are creating it for? And the answer is not 'everyone'. (Though, if I had a dollar for every time I heard the answer 'everyone', I would be very rich indeed!)

'Everyone' is not your market; 'everyone' is not your ideal client. Even some of the biggest brands in the world would never claim to have everyone as their customers. They are very clear about the characteristics of their ideal client.

What do you know about the type of person who needs your product or service?

The more you know about your client, the more you will be able to connect with them through your marketing, advertising and social media platforms, and so on, to let them know how your product and/or service is the one designed specifically with them in mind.

Ultimately, you want to be able to map out a day in the life of your client. Every small detail will increase your ability to connect with them.

Right now, as I write this book, I have two photos on the wall beside my desk – photos of my two ideal clients. In fact, these are the two people I write all my material for: my blogs, my articles, my newsletters. When I make videos, I am speaking directly to them. I know these two people as well as I know my family and close friends. These two people are the reason my business exists. I know their dreams, their plans, their pain ... and everything I do is to help them lay foundations so they have the greatest chance for success in their startup businesses.

Over time, they have become as real to me as if they were actual clients. They are avatars – hybrid characters I have created so that it is easier for me to communicate with all my clients.

An avatar needs to be really specific. A common mistake I see people make is to create a customer avatar that is too broad and general. I often hear from business owners, 'My product is for ... stay-at-home mums ... baby boomers ... Gen X ... dog lovers ...' These are way too broad and are examples of just one particular aspect of your client.

Many are terrified of being too specific because they have the belief that they will alienate other potential clients. This is not the case. In fact, the opposite is true. Many other people will also buy your product or service.

As I've said, the main reason you want to identify your ideal client is so that you can communicate with them directly. The more you know about them and the clearer you are about who they are, the easier it will be able to find them and inform them about your business and your fabulous products and services.

Knowing about your ideal client influences product design, product distribution, price, how you market, where you market – it influences every single aspect of your business.

This chapter is devoted to identifying who this person is and what they are really looking for. You may think it strange that it sounds like I'm talking about one person, but I *am* talking about one person. When you are super clear about the identity of your ideal client, your business will fly.

Here's something to watch out for, though. When you find them, you may be surprised that what they are looking for is not exactly what you are selling. What do I mean by this? I believe one of the best examples of the difference between what people buy and the value they seek comes from the weight-loss industry. A client buys a weight-loss program. They pay money for little boxes of food to be delivered to their house every week. But they are not buying little boxes of food.

They are buying a new self. They are buying confidence. They are paying to improve their health. They are buying beauty, desirability, self-esteem ... The list goes on. The weight-loss companies know this well. They know they are not selling little boxes of food.

By the end of this chapter, you will have created your ideal client avatar. You'll know all the details of their life, including what they are really looking for and the true value of what you're selling them.

IDENTIFYING YOUR IDEAL CLIENT

I'm guessing that, at some stage in your working life, you have already had clients whom you have considered your favourites. Now, it's our little secret that you like some clients more than others and they're easy to spot:

- A particular client walks in and you think, 'Nice to see you.' Maybe you even say it out loud to them.

- You see their name on an order form and you think, 'I'm going to do this order first.'

- The phone rings and when you hear who it is, you want to take that call.

- An email arrives from them in your inbox and you read their email before all the others.

- You notice they are scheduled to come into the business later in the week and you check your roster to make sure you are working that day.

Let's call this person Sarah. When you see her, or her name, you smile a little and you feel, well, that feeling we feel when someone we really like to work with has walked into our day.

Take a minute to think about Sarah and consider what it is that makes her easier to work with than all the others. Who is she and why do you like working with her? What is it about her that makes her special?

I'm going to guess it has something to do with some or all of the following ways that Sarah behaves as a client:

- She's easy to deal with.

- She knows what she wants.

- She orders the same thing every time.

- She always turns up on time.

- She's always prepared.

- If she's going away, she lets you know.

- She knows when her next appointments are.

- She pays on the day; she has the right money.

- She always pays in full and doesn't haggle for discounts.

- She refers friends to the business.

- She makes helpful suggestions.

- She likes to know about any new products.

- She says, 'Thank you.'

You wish everyone was just like Sarah, and perhaps some of your other clients are. But can you imagine having a business where everyone is like Sarah? If you follow the steps in the rest of this chapter, you will discover how to identify and find the Sarah clients for your business.

CREATING AN IDEAL CLIENT AVATAR

A profile is a description of the person who is your ideal client. It has become popular to refer to this profile as an ideal client avatar.

The ideal client avatar is made up of all the aspects of this ideal client. To help us cover all the various aspects, we look at four key areas:

1. Geographic segmentation
2. Demographic profile
3. Psychographic profile
4. Behaviour profile.

GEOGRAPHIC SEGMENTATION

This refers to the physical location of your ideal client. The best way to explain this is by example. For a café in an inner-city suburb, the geographic profile of your ideal client could be: lives within 5km of the café. A university might have a geographic profile: anyone in Australia and South East Asia.

The iconic: anywhere in the world where goods can be delivered.

For some businesses, knowing the physical location of their clients is much more important than for others.

When you think about your business idea, where will your clients come from? How far are they from your business? How do they get to your business?

Do you deliver to them? How far do you deliver? How far do you need to be able to reach?

I live in an inner-Sydney suburb where there is an amazing range of cafés, wine bars and restaurants. I regularly eat at a favourite local restaurant because I live within walking distance. That makes it easy. This business depends on customers coming back regularly and they know that geographic profile is important. I am their ideal client.

Now, you are probably thinking, 'Yes, you walk to the restaurant, but there will be people who come from other suburbs who drive.' This is certainly true. This particular restaurant has a second ideal client who lives driving distance away. As your business develops, you will identify multiple ideal clients. I strongly suggest, however, that you start with just one for now to keep things simple.

DEMOGRAPHIC PROFILE

The demographics are all the facts about a range of areas of a person's life. Think about your ideal customer in relation to the following:

- How old are they?

- Are they male or female?

- Where do they live? Which suburb?

- Are they in a house? Or flat? Or apartment?

- How many rooms do they have?

- Whom do they live with?

- Are they single? In a relationship? Are they married?

- Do they have children?

- Do they have pets?

- What do they look like? Tall, short, thin, fat, long hair, short hair, blonde, brunette, blue eyes, brown eyes, glasses, contacts?

- What clothes do they wear? Modern? New? Second-hand? Retro?

- Are they working full-time? Part-time?

- What is their educational level?

- Where were they born?

It will take a bit of time for you to answer all of these questions in relation to your ideal client. For now, you will probably have to make an educated guess or use information from previous experience to start to piece together the answers.

Some businesses create a male ideal client avatar and a female ideal client avatar. If you could find this helpful, answer these questions in relation to Sarah and then in relation to Steve.

What I often see people do when they think about demographic profile is think in terms of a range. When asked, 'What gender and how old is your ideal client?' they say, 'They are women between thirty and fifty years.'

Now, that's a lot of women. We actually want to narrow the profile as much as possible. That way, when we are talking to our ideal client, they can hear what we say.

Think about how you would talk to a thirty-year-old woman compared to a fifty-five-year-old about your business. Would it *really* be the same? Or is your business more geared towards the thirty-year-old woman? There might just be a few fifty-five-year-olds who occasionally buy from you.

If you are trying to talk to everyone, no one ends up hearing what you say because it's too generic.

One of my client's is a chiropractor. When we started working together, she told me her ideal client was 'anyone with a spine'. Now, we know that not everyone with a spine needs chiropractic services, so I challenged her to hone in her favourite clients. We looked through her current clients, using the above questions, and some more that we are going to look at in the next section, and she immediately identified the clients whom she most liked working with. She named these her ideal clients.

These are the characteristics she identified:

- They were mostly female – although not all.

- They were aged between forty and forty-five years of age.

- They were married.

- They had two children, between eight and twelve years of age.

- They cared about their health because they want to enjoy time with their family.

- They mostly worked desk jobs.

- Interestingly, they were mostly accountants and lawyers.

Once she was able to get specific and honest about whom she most wanted to treat clinically, she found the clarity and the words to connect with them. She was able to find more of them, to talk to them when they came to see her, to treat them in her unique chiropractic way. Just knowing the profile of her ideal client meant a huge shift in her thinking and in the way she then attracted and retained the clients she loved to work with in her practice.

PSYCHOGRAPHIC PROFILE

This aspect of a profile refers to traits such as lifestyle and personality. It includes people's opinions, attitudes, interests, emotions, values, social class and so on. Looking at psychographic profile is becoming increasingly important as businesses and brands seek to differentiate themselves from each other.

Overall, these factors are somewhat intangible in nature. These are the sorts of questions you would ask about your ideal client:

- How do they spend their time? At weekends? In the evenings?

- What do they like to drink?

- What do they like to eat?

- Where do they go on holidays? On weekends away?

- Do they play sport? Do they watch sport? Which sport?

- What technology do they use?

- Where do they like to shop? How do they like to pay when they are shopping?

- What sort of movies do they like?

- Do they go to a book club?

- What makes them happy? Sad? Angry? Joyful?

- Whom do they enjoy spending time with?

Eventually, you will be marketing to your ideal clients. Knowing how they access information is going to be essential because this helps you to decide where you will share information about your products and services. Here are some more key questions to consider:

- What books do they read?

- What blogs might they read?

- Do they read magazines? Which ones?

- What about newspapers? Do they subscribe online? Or read the physical item?

- Are they on LinkedIn? Facebook? Instagram? Snapchat?

One of my favourite questions to consider is: where/how do they find out what's going on in the world? Increasingly, we know that more and more people find out what's going on in the world through various forms of social rather than traditional media.

An interesting way to consider these questions is to add 'and no one else would' to each of the answers. For example: my ideal client would read [book name] and no one else would. You are looking to be as specific as you can.

One of the techniques that can be very useful is to make assumptions when you don't have data or information. An assumption is an educated guess based on the facts available to you at this point in time. We will add checking these assumptions to your list of things to do when you start your research.

The psychographic aspects are what you are tapping into when you identify your 'why' and your underpinning philosophy, which we discussed in the first chapter. These qualities may be harder to discern, so you have to dig under the surface data.

Let me give you an example. Last year, I went on a holiday on a dhoni, a traditional local boat, in the Maldives. It was eight days of complete joy on and in the water. There were five guests on that boat. At first, it looked as if we were all completely different. We came from different countries: the UK, USA, Italy, Australia. We were different ages, from early twenties to mid–fifties. We worked in completely different fields: anaesthetist, school psychologist, accountant, IT expert, business coach. However, as we got to know each other, we found similarities that were aspects of our psychographic profiles and our personal values. These were what made us ideal clients for the holiday organisers.

Earlier, we looked at the values that are important to you. In this section, you need to start to think about the values that are important to your clients.

Think about your ideal client: what are their values? What are the things that are really important to them? What are the things they won't compromise on?

Interestingly, the answers you give for your ideal client are likely to be similar to your own.

Years ago, I met with someone who wanted me to be a consultant for their company. They were the Australian branch of a US company. Our meeting had been scheduled for what turned out to be the morning of the September 11 attacks in the US in 2001. I remember driving to my meeting listening to the news on the radio and, like almost everyone else, being shocked and distressed at what had happened. When I arrived, the two men I was meeting were super excited about the prospect of how much money another division of their company was about to make. At this early stage, no one really knew what had happened, nor why. But they realised the 9/11 incident meant there would be war, and this other division supplied the goods and services needed in a war zone. Their excitement was palpable.

I personally found their behaviour and opinions completely repugnant and incongruent with my values. I couldn't believe someone could be so excited about making a lot of money out of a war. I just couldn't imagine working with or for them or having anything to do with them or their business. The meeting was much shorter than planned and I never followed up. Yes, it meant I didn't get that contract. But it also meant I was able to stay true to my values, and sleep at night.

I'm sure many of you reading this have found yourself in a similar situation where you've been faced with people with conflicting values. Being clear about your values and your 'why' makes it very easy to identify clients who are similar and clients who are not. Sometimes, it's not worth working with clients who aren't going to value your way of working because of key differences when it comes to this part of their profile.

Increasingly, environmental issues are an area where people differ in their opinions and values. They have become an important aspect of decision-making when it comes to purchasing. You can see this with the rise of conscious clothing brands. Surfing legend Kelly Slater has created a range of men's clothing that is entirely ethically sourced and manufactured. And, recently, I met the team at Little Yellow Bird, a corporate uniform supplier that uses ethically sourced fabrics to manufacture quality uniforms under fair trade working conditions.

These businesses know that their customers care where their products come from. Their ideal client wants to know that they are ethically sourced and that the people who make them have received fair trade value for their contribution.

Is the environment a key concern of your ideal client?

BEHAVIOUR PROFILE

This aspect of the profile of your ideal client is all about how they behave; specifically, their buying behaviour. Understanding the behaviour profile of your ideal client is useful for determining their buying patterns and how you might make changes to their buying patterns.

Let's look at a couple of examples that help illustrate this aspect of the ideal client. If your business idea is to open a café, one of the key behaviours you would want for your ideal client would be for them to buy a coffee every morning from your café. The buying behaviour is to buy every day. Another example might be a Pilates studio. You might want your clients to book one session every week. If your business idea is to grow herbs and sell them at the monthly farmers' markets, the buying behaviour of your ideal client would be to visit the markets every month to buy herbs, along with other organic foods and produce.

The behaviour profile looks at the difference between first-time buyers and repeat customers. When it comes to repeat purchases, this is the aspect of your ideal client that helps you to understand why they buy your product or service over and over. Why do they keep coming back? For example, I eat breakfast two to three times a week at the same café. Why? One of the biggest factors is convenience, however, there are a few other reasons that are much more important than convenience. The coffee is very good, the breakfast and coffee are affordable, everyone in the café knows me and knows how I like both my coffee and my breakfast, and they fuss to make sure it is just how I like it. Of course, there are other places I could go, but I'm never going anywhere else. Why would I? This business knows why people keep coming back to them – it's their high standard of food and terrific customer service.

Formal loyalty programs are an example of how to influence the buying behaviour of customers. I just this afternoon bought a packet of tea from our local tea shop and they asked if I was a member. They signed me up and stamped my card. After ten packets, I get one free. My pet supplies company uses my mobile phone number to track how many bags of cat food I purchase, again with the intention to influence my buying behaviour; after ten bags, I get one free and I also accrue points which give me a $10 discount at some point. The business knows that there are people who like to be rewarded for loyalty.

A repeat customer will have been a first-time buyer at some point. Right from the beginning, it is important to develop a way to ask: 'Why did you choose us?' or 'What prompted you to come to us today?' The answers to these questions will help you to build the behaviour profile of your ideal client. One of the key pieces of information you are listening for with these questions is how your potential clients have gathered their information and what it is that helps them to actually decide to purchase from you.

The sorts of things you'd be interested to understand would be in the areas of price sensitivity, brand loyalty and also hearing about the desired product benefits from your ideal client's point of view.

What are the contributing factors that take a client from a one-off, first-time purchase to becoming a loyal, repeat customer?

Again, in the planning stage, this is an area where you may have to make educated guesses about the behaviour profile of your ideal client.

Now it's time for you to start building your ideal client avatar.

Activity: Your Ideal Client Avatar

You might want to start by going back to the start of this section and thinking about Sarah or Steve, and any other similar people you have encountered in your business or imagine being in your business.

Consider the relevant questions listed in each of the key aspects of the ideal client avatar:

- Geographic segmentation

- Demographic profile

- Psychographic profile

- Behaviour profile

Answer as many as you are able based on whom you believe will be your ideal client. If you have to, make assumptions which you can test later. This is meant to be a bit of a fun exercise as well as a serious one – you're making up the perfect person!

The best thing to do is just make a start. This first avatar is a work in progress. Once you test the assumptions, you get to know your clients even better.

You can download a worksheet to help you at http://www.healthynumbers.com.au/book-templates/

Now that we know whom we're talking about, let's turn to your ideal client's problems.

WHAT PROBLEM IS YOUR IDEAL CLIENT REALLY LOOKING TO SOLVE?

In the previous section, we identified your ideal client. We now have a profile for this person, an ideal client avatar. The next step is to be really clear about what they are looking for. In many instances, what someone is looking for and what they think they are looking for are different things.

Let me give you an example. Karen buys a particular pair of sunglasses. On the surface, it might look like she is buying the sunglasses to protect her eyes from the sun because that's what sunglasses do. But those of us who know Karen know that her choice of sunglasses has much less to do with protecting her eyes from the sun and much more to do with:

- Looking up to date with the latest fashion.

- Looking like her idol who wears the same glasses.

- Hiding behind them when she is in a crowd.

- Hiding the fact she has a hangover.

You can probably think of other reasons for buying sunglasses, but you get the idea. Almost every purchase decision is made with a desire to satisfy a series of underpinning needs.

Let's look at another example: Trevor buys Sharon a bunch of flowers. The physical transaction is buying a bunch of flowers to give to Sharon. But it's not just a bunch of pretty flowers, it's:

- I'm thinking of you.

- I miss you.

- I'm sorry.

- I love you.

- Happy birthday.

- Congratulations.

And so on. Karen has bloodshot eyes from crying so she needs a pair of sunglasses. Trevor needs to say, 'I'm sorry,' and the flowers help him say that. The question for you to ask about your ideal client is: what is their core problem?

There are a number of ways to think about this question:

- What are they trying to solve?

- What are they trying to get done?

- Thinking beyond the goals that your product or service might help them with, what are their big goals?

- What is their pain point?

The reason it is important to understand this aspect of your ideal client is that you are then able to communicate to them that you have a solution for their issue. The clearer you are about their issue, the easier it will be for your client to see your product/service as the solution.

You might wondering, 'How do I figure out what the problems are for my clients?' Remember back in Chapter 2 when we looked your business idea and broadly what problem you are aiming to solve? Now you can be more specific as you think about your ideal client and their specific problems.

The best way to find out this information is to ask and listen. Listen to conversations around you. Put yourself in the position or in the environment of your ideal clients and listen to what they talk about and how they describe their issues. Make note of the exact language they use. You will use this in your marketing, on your website, in blogs and when it comes to other promotional material.

Another great way to find out about the problems and challenges of your ideal clients is to join forums where they hang out. Subscribe to their blogs and join their Facebook pages. You will learn a lot from listening in.

If you have the resources, you could set up a focus group. A focus group is where you bring together a group of people who are likely to be your ideal clients and ask them questions. Think of a list of questions that would help you to understand their situation. Ask the questions and listen to their responses.

Some years ago, a client had an idea for a fold-up shoe. Her idea was that it would be the pair you have on hand when your feet are sore from wearing high heels all day, or all night. Cynthia set up focus groups with friends and asked each person to bring another friend. The first focus group she held was to find out when women might use such a shoe. In what circumstances did women find themselves wishing they had flat shoes? What might those flat shoes be like? Where would they come from? She was also looking for some details about potential design.

Cynthia's original idea was that she would sell her flat shoes to women who would then keep them in their handbag, just in case. Very early on in the focus group, Cynthia learned that most women would not carry spare normal-sized shoes for a variety of reasons; small handbags don't fit a spare pair of shoes, and they felt that the spare pair would always be in the bag that was at home – a bit like their umbrella. They also didn't know what to do with the high heels they were wearing. The focus group gave Cynthia a great deal of useful information as she designed her fold-up shoe.

As the product prototype, the sample, started to take shape, she continued to hold focus groups to gauge the response.

If you consider holding a focus group, it's worth noting that the ideal size is between eight and twelve people who are close to your ideal client. The idea is to listen. It's good to have your questions thought through beforehand. If you are asking friends, you may need to invite them to be really honest with their responses, and double check that they do, in fact, represent your ideal client. Remember, this is a business activity. When a business conducts official focus groups, they pay their people. You may find your friends are happy with a nice cup of tea (or glass of wine) and tasty snacks as all the reward they require. If you are super excited about your business, in my experience, people just want to help you be successful. This is why it is important for them to be honest and not just say what they think you want to hear.

This is not an aspect of your business that you look at once and then consider set in stone. Over time, you will continue to gather information about the problems faced by your clients as your business continues to provide the solution they are looking for.

This brings me to you the next stage, which is a close examination of how they currently solve their problem.

HOW DOES YOUR IDEAL CLIENT SOLVE THEIR PROBLEM AT THE MOMENT?

In the previous chapter, we looked at the competition in your industry, both direct and indirect. If you completed the activity, you will have identified who, in general, makes up your direct and indirect competition; what they do that makes them successful; why people choose their product/service; what is not being offered in the industry; and what you can do to differentiate your business from the others.

This section is going to take a slightly different slant on competition. We know who your ideal client is and we know what their problem is. Now we are going to ask: how do they solve their problem right now?

Imagine you are a Pilates instructor. Your ideal client is someone who is recovering from a running injury. Their problem consists of the fact that:

- They are in pain.

- They cannot run right now.

How are they solving the problem right now? There are a number of potential ways they could be addressing the issue at the moment:

- Seeing a physio for treatment.

- Using heat packs or ice packs.

- Not running at all.

- Running through the pain.

- Doing nothing.

- Using pain relief ointments/creams.

- Seeing an acupuncture clinician.

As you can see, in this example, some of the ways they choose to solve the problem will have more favourable outcomes than others! Remember, 'do nothing' is unlikely to be a solution to a problem. Eventually, we have to do something. That said, there will always be potential clients who do nothing for a very long time.

We can use this information to find ways to communicate with our ideal client. Again, this forms part of your marketing strategy.

For example, if you are this Pilates instructor and you believe that one of the ways your ideal client is currently solving their problem is by visiting a physiotherapist, then part of your marketing strategy would be to develop relationships with your local physiotherapists.

Chapter 7 is focussed on your marketing plan and all of this information about your ideal client comes into play. I see so many businesses rush out to build a website and spend money on advertising. Then I watch them wonder why it doesn't bring them the results they hoped for. We call that 'Hope Marketing'.

There is no point spending any money on your website, marketing or advertising if you are not clear about:

- Your ideal client.

- Their core problem.

- How they solve it now.

- Your true value – which we will look at in the next section.

Activity: Your Ideal Client's Current Solution

Think about your ideal client and the problem they have, and ask yourself: how do they solve their problem right now? Make a list, as in the Pilates example, and consider the question from a range of perspectives.

When you know how your ideal client currently solves their problem, you are better able to educate them about how and why your solution is better than their current solution. This is the 'true value' of your business.

WHAT'S YOUR TRUE VALUE?

Let me describe a scenario maybe some of you will relate to. It's 4pm and I receive a text: 'What's for dinner?' I pause, my shoulders slump, I sigh and I reply with one of three of my homemade dinner menu options. I have a small repertoire. This is seriously one of the most dreaded questions in my day.

Core problem: what to have for dinner?

How I solve it: one of three home-cooked options – or eat out or get take away.

This comes with a lot of feelings of frustration. I love food and cooking and eating. What I do not like is the 'What's for dinner?' question.

Hello Fresh is a business that knows this scenario plays out in hundreds, if not thousands, of households around Australia, and it offers a solution. Once a week, Hello Fresh delivers to homes across the country the box containing fresh pre-portioned ingredients with instructive recipe cards for making each dish.

We pay the company a fixed dollar amount each week. But what is the true value of the box? It is so much more than the sum of the contents: the ingredients, the spices, the vegetables, the recipes and so on.

The true value for me is in answering the 'What's for dinner?' question and providing the exact ingredients to make healthy and nutritious meals at home. Hello Fresh knows this.

There are other reasons it works really well, which provide added value:

- The shopping is done for you, which saves time and energy.

- You get only the ingredients you need, which reduces waste and saves money.

- The recipe cards are super easy to follow.

- The meal portions are generous without being too much.

- There is variety because each week the menu changes.

Now, just to let you know, I do not own shares or receive any financial incentive from Hello Fresh to talk about the company. I just find it such a great example of providing true value that I have to rave a little!

You now know who your ideal client is, what their problem is and what they are currently doing to solve it. When you consider your business and the solution that you offer, ask yourself: what is the true value that I offer to my clients that they are not already getting from their current solution?

If we go back to the Pilates example: the ideal client is an injured runner who is seeing a physiotherapist. By adding Pilates to the rehabilitation, the Pilates instructor's true value is in the following:

- Pilates can help build a base of strength and stability so the runner can return to running with ease.

- Since Pilates is a non-impact exercise, it's ideal for runners who are injured.

- Pilates was developed as a rehabilitation exercise for WWI soldiers allowing them to rehabilitate while bedridden.

Imagine you are that Pilates instructor and you are writing a blog about the impact of Pilates on recovery from a running injury. Would your ideal patient understand the true value of adding Pilates to their recovery program? What if the physiotherapist explained these benefits to the patient and then recommended they contact you?

The ideal client would be much more likely to contact the Pilates instructor with a positive and receptive frame of mind in awareness of the true value of Pilates for their running recovery.

One of the ways to think about true value is to think about how the life of your client will improve when they use your product or service. The runner will get back to running more quickly and with a greater base of stability, so preventing further injury. Hello Fresh knows it improves my life and the lives of all its customers with that box of healthy food and the recipe cards delivered every week by making it easy to put a healthy meal on the table. How do you improve the lives of your clients?

Activity: Your True Value

Make a list of all the ways your solution provides value to your ideal client. What is your true value? Think back to the Hello Fresh and Pilates examples. How can you emulate what they deliver to their ideal clients?

The more you know and understand your ideal client, what they are truly looking for and how you solve that with value that they cannot get anywhere else, the greater the likelihood of your business being successful.

Linking what you've learned about yourself, your idea and your clients together is how you form an unbeatable brand.

4. YOUR BRAND

'You've either got or you haven't got style,
and if you've got it stand out a mile.'

FRANK SINATRA

What is a brand? Many people think of the logo, the tagline or the music that goes with a particular business. But brand is actually bigger than that. It is the overall story of a business and its owner(s). It's the promise or the essence of what the client will experience. It involves values and reputation. A brand is developed over time.

It's important to think about your brand right from the beginning because, as you establish your business, your brand develops along with you. Your story is part of your brand. When your ideal clients hear your story, they will be attracted to you and your business.

Large companies spend a fortune on attracting customers and creating brand loyalty, but a brand isn't just for Big Business. Your brand is what separates you from your competitors and helps your customers remember who you are regardless of your size.

DEVELOPING A CLEAR BRAND

These are the seven steps to creating and implementing a clear brand (you'll notice we've already covered a couple of these steps!):

1. Define who you are and what you do.

2. Stand for something – your 'why'.

3. Define your ideal client.

4. Connect with your audience.

5. Adopt a 'voice' for your business that reflects your brand.

6. Create collateral: your logo, business name, tagline, colours, photographs and so on.

7. Be consistent – stay true to your brand.

DEFINE WHO YOU ARE AND WHAT YOU DO

Right at the beginning, we identified who you are and what you do. You defined your product/service and tested your business idea. You also considered how you are different to everyone else and how you and your business stand out from your competition.

STAND FOR SOMETHING – YOUR 'WHY'

In the first chapter, you looked at what makes up your Golden Circle. More than just what you do, this considers your underpinning 'why' and 'how' you do things – your values. This is what you stand for. One of the roles of a brand is to inspire.

DEFINE YOUR IDEAL CLIENT

We also looked in detail at your ideal client and created an ideal client avatar. Brand is all about story – and you know their story. You identified the problem your client has and what they are really looking for.

When we talk about the essence of your brand, it's how your customers will feel when they interact with you. When you know who you are, what you do, what you stand for and whom you're talking to, it influences your communication style.

CONNECTING WITH YOUR AUDIENCE

You've probably been where your customer is at some point – you know how they feel. Often, the reason someone starts a business is that they couldn't find what they need or what they did find didn't quite work for them. I have a client who cares about the environment, so much so that when she realised how many plastic bags she was using in the fruit and vegetable section of the supermarket, she decided to make her own reusable gauze bags. One thing led to another and now she has a website with an online store, Facebook and Instagram accounts, and she sends her Fruity Sacks all over the world. You may want to check it out here www.fruitysacks.com

Leandra connects with her audience by letting them know the benefits of the reusable bag versus the singe-use plastic bag. She knows that her customers feel the same way she does about those single-use plastic bags. She knows the language to use to connect with them, because she knows how they feel, because it's how she feels.

When you know who your ideal clients are, it becomes easier to decide how to connect with them.

What will they hear? What will resonate for them? No one wants to be shouted at. Don't just yell, 'Buy my stuff.' When connecting with your audience, you want to make them feel like you know them, you understand their problems, you care about them so much that you have created this solution – just for them.

Connecting with your audience is about the emotional relationship you have with them. Emotions are the primary driver of most of our purchasing decisions. How do you improve the emotional relationship you have with your clients? Here are four aspects to effectively connect with your audience:

SPEAK TO THEM ONE-TO-ONE

This is your ideal client. Imagine you are having a cup of tea with them, or a coffee, or you are out for a walk together. How do you talk to them? What do you say? This is about them, not about you. The most important aspect of this is that the person listening to what you are saying or reading what you have written feels like you are talking to them, just them.

HAVE SOMETHING INTERESTING AND UNIQUE TO SAY

Your clients want to feel like they come to you for something they cannot hear anywhere else. Take a unique or quirky position on some aspect of your industry that resonates with your audience. For example, when Paul Lindley founded Ella's Kitchen in the UK in 2006, he wanted to create a food business that was more than just about baby food and profit; he wanted to encourage kids to develop healthier eating habits. This made Ella's Kitchen stand out from the other baby food companies at the time

LET YOUR CLIENT AND YOUR AUDIENCE BE THE HERO

You may have heard that storytelling is one way to connect with your clients. Think about a great story where the hero goes through a transformation, overcomes obstacles or develops a skill. It is easy in the business world to feel like we are rescuing the clients by providing them with the solution to their problem. But most people want to feel like *they* are the hero. Every hero needs a guide, a coach, a Sherpa, and that is the role you can play. So our role as the business owner is to communicate in such a way that our clients feel like they are the hero. Make your clients the heroes and you will find that other people want to take the same journey with you.

I believe that Leandra and her Fruity Sacks are a terrific example of this. Her customers feel like heroes when they don't use a plastic bag at the supermarket; they feel like they are saving the planet and the oceans. I know I certainly do.

USE HUMOUR, COMPASSION AND EMPATHY. ABOVE ALL, BE AUTHENTIC

I'm not funny and I never try to be because it just doesn't work. However, others do it very well and manage to connect with their audience through humour. What I am is enormously compassionate and empathetic to a wide variety of people and their circumstances. Understanding your audience and being able to be empathetic to their situation can be part of the true value they will gain from buying your products and services. One of the ways that a business can demonstrate this is to give examples of previous clients or situations and emphasise their compassionate response to those clients' experiences.

However you connect with your audience, authenticity is vital. Most clients can detect when someone is genuine and when they are not. Meanwhile, the Internet and social media have made it much easier to detect when someone is less than authentic. Would you want to deal with a business you suspect doesn't mean what they say?

Activity: Connecting with Your Audience

You may find it interesting to observe how these four aspects apply to you and your own interaction with the various brands that try to communicate with you. Do you feel as if the brand is talking to you specifically? Do they say something quirky or unique? Do you feel like a hero? Are they empathetic to your situation?

Take each of the above aspects and identify how these could be applied to your business idea.

Over time, you may come across other ways to connect effectively with your audience. For now, these are a great start. Next, we're going to look at the 'voice' you use.

ESTABLISHING THE VOICE OF YOUR BUSINESS

This is such an important aspect of brand. Your 'voice' is what will allow you to communicate in a way that makes people want to work with you again and again, and refer you to others.

How do you sound when you speak? Your goal is to build affinity and connection with your clients. When you sound the way they do, they feel comfortable – it feels familiar. For example, if your business idea is to make and sell children's educational toys, your target audience will be parents, and maybe grandparents, so your voice may be a mixture – fun, serious, bubbly, off-the-cuff, straightforward, anecdotal and so on. You may aim to be more like one parent talking to another or talking to a good friend.

Think about your audience: are they formal? Or more casual? Again, when you know your ideal clients, you know their 'voice'.

A useful exercise is to create a brand voice chart. This is different to a writing style guide, which covers specifics like grammar, punctuation, font, spelling and so on. The brand voice chart sets out the tone of the style of writing. There are three steps:

Step 1: Use three words to describe your brand personality. If you thought about your brand as a person and you were telling someone else about that person, what three words would you use? For my brand, my three words are:

- Passionate

- Straightforward

- Empathetic

Step 2: Elaborate a bit further on what these words mean when describing the personality (voice) of your business. For my business:

- Passionate = enthusiastic, expressive, energetic

- Straightforward = honest, clear, forthright, simple, sincere

- Empathetic = caring, sensitive, compassionate

Step 3: Add a brief description of what each word means, then add the Dos and Don'ts of each aspect of your voice. You can see an extract from my business brand voice chart below:

So You Want to Start a Business™

Brand Voice Chart

Voice Characteristics	Description	Do	Don't
Passionate	We're passionate about changing the way people get started in business	Use strong verbs Be a champion for business startups	Be wishy washy Use passive voice Use past tense – unless essential

Energetic (secondary characteristic of Passionate)	We want to convey a sense of energy and moving on with our actions	Use action words Convey a sense of urgency	Find ways to make excuses
Straightforward	We want people to be able to understand what we are talking about	Use simple English Say what we mean Keep it simple	Overcomplicate things

Check the tone of voice of your competitors. How will you sound different? It is very easy to sound just the same as others in your industry. You have the option to sound completely different, so your ideal clients can find you in a sea of sameness.

Activity: Your Brand Voice Chart

Follow the three steps and create the brand voice chart for your business idea. You can download a template here: http://www.healthynumbers. com.au/book-templates/

The next stage is to think about the collateral you're going to use to share your brand with your audience.

CREATING COLLATERAL

This is often seen as the fun stuff – the place most people want to start! Putting together effective collateral for your business is a big job and drawing a logo and choosing the colours is only part of it.

Collateral is the tangible media used to promote the brand and support sales and marketing. It's the media that your audience will come into contact with, whether physically, with something they can touch in real life, or virtually, online.

Collateral is important because it encompasses the things that your audience will associate with your business. So what sort of collateral do you need for your business? And how do you create that collateral?

Creating collateral will be an ongoing task in your business. You may choose to outsource it to a brand collateral expert, however it's worth having a go yourself, partly so you know what is involved and also so you are more knowledgeable when seeking professional assistance.

Creating collateral is quite straightforward. There are four steps:

Step 1: Define your objectives. When you create a piece of collateral, it is important to know:

- Who the target is – new clients, existing clients, lapsed clients

- What the purpose is – inform, increase brand awareness, introduce a new product and so on.

Step 2: Know your audience. We have already talked about having an ideal client avatar. You must be starting to see how often this comes up. It's involved in every aspect of your brand and marketing efforts.

Step 3: Grab their attention. Whatever collateral item you create, your audience needs to be engaged within seconds. What will you do to grab the attention of your audience?

Step 4: Measure the impact. Everything needs to be measured for impact. If you post a blog, how many people read it? If you run an advert, how many people click through to your website?

With these four steps in mind, here is a list of potential collateral items to consider for your business. Of course, you do not need to have each and every one of these right now. Choose the ones that will be most suitable for your business and your audience. I take a few critical examples and examine them in more detail at the end of the list.

Business name	You may choose to trade under your own name or choose a name that encapsulates your business.
Website	This is your digital home. It can be the most important piece of collateral for attracting clients.
Business fact sheet	This includes the date your business was founded, your contact information, your address, your social media links and so on.
Product/service fact sheet	This states the key features, benefits, specifications, reliability.
Mission statement	This can be for your clients as well as internal use.
Biographies of the founder and other relevant people	The 'About' page is one of the most visited pages on most websites for small businesses. People want to know who they are dealing with.
Testimonials	Reviews from existing clients can be collected on Google and Facebook and added to your website.
Client list	Being willing to display your client list builds trust. It is helpful to potential clients, investors, suppliers and prospective employees.
Case studies	These stories are the best way to demonstrate to potential clients similar work that you have done in the past.
Q&A for prospecting calls	Being able to answer questions confidently demonstrates to prospective clients that you know them well and understand their situation. Make a list of the sorts of questions you are frequently asked and prepare answers; update this list as you are asked new questions. It can be helpful to add FAQs (Frequently Asked Questions) to your website.
Letter templates	If your business sends out letters, having standard formats and templates helps establish a professional image for the brand.
Email templates	If you are sending out regular emails, it gives your clients confidence when they recognise a consistent format. Emails are a very effective way to stay in contact with clients. The key to truly effective emails is to provide value in terms of useful information and items of interest to your audience.

Style guide	This contains the theme elements of your brand: key graphics, colours, logo, fonts, phrases and brand-oriented words.
Videos	Video is becoming increasingly important in demonstrating, communicating and reinforcing brand awareness. You can make videos about your products and the features of the value you provide.
Blog content	If your business audience finds blog content useful, it can be an important part of your brand collateral.
White papers	These can be used to set you and your business apart as a thought leader. They can be sold or used as free gifts for potential clients.
e-books	These are among the most commonly used collateral. They can communicate information and be used to collect contact details before they are made available.
Press kit	There will be times when you will want to send out a press kit, for example, at the launch of your business or launch of new products or other significant event. A press kit includes items such as your logo, business fact sheets, product fact sheet, client list, case studies, your business card, business clippings and more.
Social media content	There are so many platforms to consider when it comes to social media. It is worth setting up accounts on platforms your ideal clients frequent and engaging with them there.
Business cards	Even today, when it can feel like everything is digital, having a business card can still be useful.
Brochures and flyers	Depending on how you target your audience, physical media may still have a role to play.

Let's now look a little closer at a few of the key items.

BUSINESS NAME

What will you call your business? If you opt to be a sole trader in Australia or a sole proprietor in the US, you can operate under your own name. You can also choose to register a business trading name. I chose the name Healthy Numbers many years ago because I believe that it describes what I believe is important in business. All the numbers need to be healthy in order for a business to be successful. How does your business name reflect what your business stands for?

When choosing a name for your business, here are some key questions to consider:

1. How does the name sound when someone says it out loud? Someone named Richard, known to everyone as Dick, started a cleaning business called Dick Cleaners and Carpet Services. He added the Carpet Services so that it sounded better. I'm not sure how successful he was.

2. Does it always sound the same? Is it one of those words or names where people wonder, 'How do you pronounce that?' or 'How do you spell that?' A new cake shop has opened near us called Saga (after the lead character in *The Bridge* a Nordic TV series produced in 2013). I've heard people refer to it as 'that new cake shop, the one with the name you don't know how to pronounce'. For some businesses, that might be their point of difference, but I find it's generally better to go with something everyone knows how to say.

3. What does the name look like when it's written down? On paper, on your website? How will it look as part of a logo? Usually, something with not too many words works best for a logo.

4. What does it say about you and your business? Does it describe what you do? I was recently talking to a marketing expert and he said, 'If it says tomato soup on the can, you want tomato soup *in* the can.' One of my favourite examples of this is a local tailor named Take Up Pants. We all know what he does.

5. What connotations does it evoke for your clients? For your potential clients? For your team? Is it the sort of name that everyone will feel represents their relationship with your business?

6. Does it represent your niche? Does the name reflect the outcome your clients will achieve? I work with a lot of health and wellness businesses and recently I came across a Pilates studio named Free

Movement Pilates. That pretty much describes the outcome that the clients will experience.

7. Can you obtain the URL for this business name? You need the URL for your website. What about all the other social media channels? It is becoming more and more difficult to come up with a name that both meets the necessary aspects of the business *and* is available online. Check for the URL. It may be necessary to look at a .net or .biz for your website address. Check if the name is available across various social media channels and even if you are not planning to use a particular social media channel at the start, grab the name so that it's yours.

WEBSITE, WEBHOST AND URL

If you're wondering whether you need a website, the answer is probably 'yes'. I like to think of my website as being the online home for my business; it's where everything is.

Even having a simple one- or two-page website creates an online presence. A website increases your credibility because it gives you a platform to share information and let people know who you are, what your business does and what you stand for.

So what do you actually need to do to create a website? Three things. You need the domain name or the URL, you need a webhost, and then you need the actual content of the website.

I talked about the domain name, the URL, in the previous section. These are the words, usually your business name, that make up the address of your website.

The next step is to decide where to host your website. A webhost is a company that provides space on a server where your website will reside. They will charge an annual or monthly fee. One of the best ways to decide who to choose to be your webhost is to ask others who they use or do a Google search and read the reviews. Once you choose a webhost, you then tell them your domain name and they create a space on their server. Imagine you decide to take a stall at your local farmers' market. You pay your money and they allocate you a space, probably a small tent-like stand with a table. It is then up to you to decorate and make it yours. This is similar to a webhost; they provide the space and you need to fill it with your content.

There are two main ways to create your website.

1. **Do it yourself.** Many people start off with a simple self-made website, though it's important to ask if this is actually the best use of your time. If you decide to go ahead yourself, you will likely use one of the Content Management Systems (CMS) on offer. These allow you to put pictures, content and videos on your site. The most popular CMS is WordPress. It is very easy to use and the basic version is completely free, but there are alternatives: Shopify is particularly good for ecommerce, i.e. if you are selling a physical product; Squarespace has a reputation for being user friendly and reliable; and other people prefer Wix or Weebly. Take a look at the different platforms and see what suits you best.

2. **Outsource building your website.** One option is to engage an entry-level designer to do the work for you. They can easily be found on a site called upwork.com. You post your job on the site and a number of people will respond. Next, you choose the one you believe will best do the work you need. I always recommend having a look at other websites they have done; that's a good way of gauging their skill level. Upwork also has comments and recommendations so you can check them out as well.

There are many companies that specialise in making website. And the costs will vary. If you choose to engage a web developer, it's always important to be really clear about what the expectations are and exactly what you're getting for the price. Where people are not clear about their expectations, more money is involved and things can turn sour.

I highly recommend that you separate the webhost from the web developer. There is a very good reason for this. If you have a separate webhost, your website is yours. Some developers will suggest that they both develop and host your site. I always caution against this. If anything goes wrong and the developer is your webhost, then they own your website. I know of a number of instances where new business owners have decided they want to stop working with their web developer (for any one of a number of reasons) and have had to pay large exit fees to be able to have access to their own website. You can avoid this happening by arranging your own webhosting contract and then separately engaging a web developer.

No matter who is actually creating your website, you will still need to provide the concept and most of the words, images and videos. If you have already created some of your basic collateral, this will be helpful in putting everything together.

There is a third way to create your website – asking family or friends to do it for you. I would caution you on this, however, unless you know two things: that they actually know what they are doing, and that they will agree to a clear contract, setting out your expectations. Often, the best way to get things done is to keep things professional.

SOCIAL MEDIA

There are almost 200 different social media platforms to choose from. Each attracts a different audience and is used for a different form of communication.

Today, it would be difficult to run a business and not be on at least one of the social platforms, but which to choose? I always recommend my clients focus on just one or two – at most three – social media platforms. It would be enormously time consuming – and, therefore, expensive – to try to do more.

Refer to the four steps mentioned earlier when it comes to creating your content on these platforms. Make sure that, when you spend time on social media, you:

1. Define your objectives
2. Know your audience
3. Grab their attention
4. Measure the impact.

Be really mindful of vanity metrics versus metrics that show you are converting people into actual paying clients. 'Vanity metrics' refer to the large numbers of likes or followers that pretty much give you bragging rights, but little else. A small number of loyal, engaged and committed followers can be much more valuable than hundreds of thousands of people who rarely engage and never buy anything.

Overall, when it comes to creating collateral, it can be worth considering engaging professional help. Look around at other logos, websites and so on that you like and find out who worked on them. Take real pride in your brand. When I worked at Qantas, they were hyper vigilant about protecting everything about their collateral – from the logo and the colour palette to the font and text size they use. The Qantas image is recognised around the world and they're proud of it.

CONSISTENCY

The seventh element when it comes to creating your brand is consistency. A consistent message enhances connection. The ultimate goal is to have everything look and feel the same so that when someone is exposed to your collateral, they recognise your brand instantly.

I cannot emphasise enough how important this consistency is – in everything. In the old days, you could stamp your logo on everything and that was enough; a bit like the 'brand' stamped on cattle out on the farms (that's actually where the word came from).

Now, it's so much more important to pay attention to the other elements of your brand so you can be recognised for what your brand stands for.

If it is just going to be you running your business, you may be wondering how you could be anything other than consistent. But it isn't always just you. From time to time, you will engage others in your business, and being able to communicate your brand to them will mean that they are able to present your brand as if they are you. It might be someone designing your logo, developing your website, sending out your invoices, putting together your packaging, and so much more.

Building your brand takes place over time, but it starts right now. Your brand is the essence of who you are, what you do and the clients you attract. You cannot fake it. You have to determine what your brand will be – what it will look like and sound like and what it will stand for.

A business that I believe does this extremely well is Lululemon Athletica. It is a business that makes yoga and sportswear, but it's also more than that. The business's consistent message is about actually doing the yoga, and the difference yoga has on your overall wellbeing. Lululemon Athletica hosts free yoga classes instore as well as public outdoor classes. It has yoga ambassadors. When you sign up for email, there is a thank you email with a woman in a yoga pose as the background. If you went to its website right now, you'd find yoga; the Twitter page shows the yoga banner, and the Facebook and Instagram accounts are similar. While there are a lot of other sporty activities Lululemon Athletica clothing is suitable for, there is a clear and consistent focus on yoga. And if you walk into one of its stores, it feels similar to being in its online presence. The way the team are trained to engage with the customers reflects the language on the website. Lululemon Athletica is consistent and that makes customers feel comfortable. The familiar increases confidence, making it easier for customers to decide to buy.

Once you've worked through this chapter on brand, you stand to create a brand that could be as strong for your clients as Lululemon Athletica's is for its clients.

Now that we've looked at the first four elements of a successful startup – you, your idea, your clients and your brand – it's time to address the super exciting aspects of structure, risk and compliance. This might be less interesting to some readers, but it's just as important as everything else when it comes to getting started in business.

5. YOUR STRUCTURE

'Before everything else, getting ready
is the secret of success.'

HENRY FORD

nyone familiar with Stephen R Covey's book *The 7 Habits of Highly Effective People* (1989), will immediately recognise 'Begin with the end in mind' as habit number two.

'Begin with the end in mind' is the concept of creating in your mind that which cannot yet be seen in physical reality. Almost everything we physically create is first created in our mind, whether taking a holiday, building a house or something as simple as cooking dinner; these all begin as an idea in our imagination. The same applies to starting a business.

Some of the 'end in mind' aspects of business are difficult to imagine, just as is the case with holidays and home building. You can have an idea of how you imagine it is going to be but, at the same time, it might not turn out that way.

Regardless, there are a few aspects of starting your business that require informed decisions to be made that will impact you and your business in the future.

Challenging you to imagine the future and think about what you want from your business, this chapter will help you to make decisions about the foundations to establish so that your business can support you in the way you want it to.

IS YOUR BUSINESS A 'KEEPER' OR A 'BUILD TO SELL'?

Do you want to create your business to sell? Or to franchise? Or do you imagine a business that you will work in and be part of for a long time? You may start out with a hobby that grows into a business and, there you are, an accidental business owner. Or you may start out with the idea to be in your business forever, but the opportunity to sell may present itself as too good an opportunity to refuse. There are numerous scenarios of what might be.

As I mentioned in the introduction, there is a spectrum with two basic types of business at either end. At one end is the pure Hobby/Lifestyle Business. It gives you an income doing something you really love doing, offers complete flexibility to work when you want, and generates *just* enough money to cover the costs of being in business and pay you enough to live a comfortable lifestyle – whatever that means for you.

At the other end of the spectrum is what I refer to as a Big Business. This is the full-on entrepreneurial startup with a highly-driven founder who is prepared to work twenty-five hours a day to create a business that will be sold for millions to one of the big players.

Between these extremes are all the other new business startups, which include small local businesses, social enterprises, franchises, network marketing companies, innovative app and tech companies, and high-revenue businesses catering to individualised niches. These often support employment, generate growth and contribute both to their local communities and the overall economy.

When Maryanne Shearer created the iconic business T2, she started in a single store in Melbourne in 1996. At that point, did she imagine that she would go on to sell her company and the forty company-owned Australian retail stores to multinational Unilever? Maybe. What did happen before the sale was finalised in 2013 was that the business wanted to expand and didn't have the resources to do it alone. Unilever, with its world reach, was looking for a premium tea brand to add to Lipton's range. Meanwhile, T2 saw itself in all the major cities in the world … so the discussions began.

When Peter Alexander created his sleepwear label in the 1980s, did he plan to sell the brand to the Just Group? I don't think so. The business environment changed and when the opportunity to sell came up, he took it.

When Jo Malone created her fragrance and candle business, did she imagine selling it to Estee Lauder? In fact, Jo Malone never intended to start a business selling perfumes and candles at all. She loved candles and making homes smell nice and her story is that of the hobby that became an empire.

In the past, when people started businesses, many of them hadn't a thought about selling for millions. However, times have changed. Today, many women and men of all ages are creating businesses with the specific intention of trying to sell for millions, or at least a tidy sum to fund a certain lifestyle.

This is particularly true of tech industries. In the past few years, we have witnessed Amazon buy Zappos, eBay buy Gumtree, and Facebook buy Instagram. Each of these deals has seen millions of dollars change hands.

Just for the record, it's worth considering the strong correlation between the amount of time, energy, commitment and resources that go into creating a business and the amount they are sold for. There is no such thing as an 'overnight success'. Each and every one of the businesses mentioned has taken years to get to the point where it's been possible for them to be sold for the amazing amounts of money that we've heard about.

Activity: Your Business Type

What type of business are you starting? Where do you see yourself on the spectrum?

You may see yourself at a particular point on the spectrum now, but also consider the future. Where do you see your business this time next year? In five years' time? In ten years' time?

Being in business is a long-term commitment, and where you see yourself heading will affect how you set yourself up at the start.

WHAT LEGAL BUSINESS STRUCTURE WILL WORK BEST FOR YOU?

This section looks at some of the legal requirements necessary to consider when setting up your business. The guidance here is general in nature because these matters can be so complex; it is best to seek legal advice from your lawyer and/or accountant before making your final decision. The money and time spent is well worth the investment – it could well save you potential issues later in your business.

How you choose to structure your business directly impacts your personal liability, your startup costs and the paperwork required, as well as the tax you pay. No one is saying that you have to be an Incorporated Pty Ltd company, however there can be advantages when it comes to financing and liability, so it's worth being aware of the options.

AUSTRALIA

First, I'm going to cover the structures available in Australia, before turning to those you might establish in the US.

Let's look at why you might want to choose one or other of these structures.

Sole Trader

If it is just you, you don't have employees and you are using your name, then being a sole trader could be an ideal choice. There are few legal and tax formalities. Setting up as a sole trader is a simple and relatively inexpensive exercise.

In Australia, you need an Australian Business Number (ABN), which is a unique eleven-digit identifying number that a business uses when dealing with other businesses. These are easily obtained online from the Australia Tax Office (ATO) website.

As a sole trader, you control and manage the whole business and are legally responsible for all aspects of the business. All income is deemed to be your income. All expenses that relate to the generation of this income can be claimed and submitted as deductions when completing your annual tax return. The net income from the business is taxed at the same rate as the individual personal income rate. All losses are deemed your losses and cannot be shared with any other person or entity. There may be limited opportunity to offset tax losses against other sources of income – you would need to check your personal circumstances with your accountant. If your business does run at a loss, there may be opportunity to carry forward that loss – again, checking your personal circumstances with your accountant is important.

(Regarding losses: Most people in business are here to make a profit. While losses do occur from time to time, our intention in this book is to focus on creating a business that will generate profit and positive cash flow – we'll talk more about this in the next chapter.)

As a sole trader, you are responsible for paying your own superannuation contributions and there is limited ability to claim the super payment as a tax deduction. Businesses operating as a sole trader find they have limited access to raising capital, bank funding or loans and to being able to enter into long-term lease or other contracts. Some years ago, a client of mine was unable to sign a property lease as a sole trader.

Something else to keep in mind as a sole trader is that you have total personal liability for financial obligations and your personal property and assets might be vulnerable if the business has financial difficulties.

When operating as a sole trader making profit, it is a good idea to set aside a portion of your revenue in preparation for paying your tax at the end of the year; a good estimate is about thirty per cent. After your first year in business, you could be asked to pay provisional PAYG (Pay As You Go) tax based on the profit you have made in the previous year. It is wise to keep funds for paying tax to avoid having to deal with a large tax bill and especially avoid paying any penalties.

Being a sole trader, you are the business, so it cannot be sold to anyone else, i.e. ownership cannot be transferred. After trading as a sole trader for a period of time, however, it is relatively simple to change business structure if you wish to do so.

Incorporated Company

As an incorporated company, the business is a distinct legal entity controlled by directors and owned by shareholders. If your business is just you, it's still possible in Australia and in New Zealand to set up a sole-director company, with you as the sole shareholder.

One of the perceived advantages of being a company is that it creates distance between the directors and personal liability. Being a company can provide limited asset protection to directors, however directors could still find themselves legally liable for their actions and the debt of the company. If a company is making a credit application to set up a credit/charge account with another business, there is often a 'directors' personal liability' clause to be completed by directors before credit application is approved. Shareholders' liability is limited to their shareholding.

Because an incorporated company has a more complex business structure, the set-up costs are higher and there are more administrative requirements, which lead to additional costs. Annual returns need to be prepared and provided to the Australian Securities and Investment Commission (ASIC). Your accountant will be able to take care of all the legislative requirements of being an incorporated company, but for a fee. This adds to the cost of being an incorporated company.

Other advantages include a potentially lower tax rate. The tax rate for small business companies is 28.5 per cent. Small businesses are those with aggregated turnover (i.e. grouped with related entities) of less than two million dollars. The general company income tax rate in Australia at the time of printing is thirty per cent. Individual PAYG rates are calculated on a sliding scale for a sole trader. If this is your key consideration in choosing between being a sole trader and being an incorporated company, it is worthwhile for you to work with your accountant to calculate your personal threshold for tax purposes.

One of the key attractions and benefits of being a company is that ownership can be transferred and/or shares sold. This means the business can be sold to another party. There is often greater opportunity to raise funds or raise capital when a business is an incorporated company.

If you are considering this structure, again, it's best to check the process with your legal advisor and/or accountant. They can take care of the set-up and legalities, though you can Google it and do it yourself using online company set-up. You just need to consider whether it's the best use of your time.

Partnership

This structure is relatively inexpensive to set up and administer. The partners share decision-making, control, income, profits, losses and debts. The partnership itself is not a legal entity and does not pay tax. Each individual is responsible for paying tax on the share of the income each receives from the partnership. There is little or no asset protection, which leaves each partner potentially liable for any debts incurred, even if only one is directly responsible for incurring the debt in question.

Having a legal and formal partnership agreement is not essential, although it is highly recommended. I remember a few years ago teaching my 'How to start a business' class and there were three young men contemplating a partnership structure for their business idea. I suggested the importance of seeking legal advice to ensure they started off with the best possible agreement. Another participant commented, 'But isn't it expensive to go to a lawyer?' It can be. But it's not nearly as expensive as it might be if you don't. The courts and mediation practices are filled with partnerships gone wrong.

I often meet people who think that a partnership is a good solution to having the necessary support to create a business. It's easy to believe that you will be best friends forever because, right now, the excitement and enthusiasm are driving and carrying you forward. When things get sticky due to difference of opinion or cash flow issues, however, it can be great to have thought through some of these things while you are in the planning stages. If you are thinking about setting up a formal partnership as your business structure, here are a few things to consider:

- Do you have the same vision for the business as the other potential partners?

- Do you have the same approach to risk?

- How are you going to apportion the workload? Who will be responsible for which tasks and operations?

- Will you set up a board?

- How will partners be made accountable for their roles?

- How will you deal with differences of opinion?

- What will be the trigger to sell or wind up the partnership or buy out the other partners?

A great resource on this subject is my podcast 'So You Want to Start a Business'. (To find the episodes you can head to iTunes podcasts and type in 'So You Want to Start a Business'.) In my very first episode, I talk with Adam Franklin, who set up a business with his Grade One best friend. All these years later, their business is flourishing and their friendship is solid.

Again, the importance of being really clear from the outset – beginning with the end in mind – applies to considering partnerships as a business structure. As I've already stated, getting good advice from a lawyer and/or accountant is critical. Choosing the right structure is important and understanding why that one is right for you is equally important.

Most people reading this book in Australia will likely be considering setting up as either a sole trader or an incorporated company. Let's summarise the advantages and disadvantages of the two structures:

Sole Trader Advantages

- Simple and low cost to set up and close down.

- Minimal legal requirements.

- Limited recording keeping and reporting.

- All financial income goes to the owner; one tax return.

- Can register a business name.

- It's easy to change to a different structure if you decide to.

Sole Trader Disadvantages

- Owner has unlimited liability for debts.

- You are taxed as a single person, i.e. PAYG rates.

- Ownership of the business cannot be transferred.

- Can have limited capacity to raise capital.

Incorporated Company Advantages

- Liability of the shareholders is limited.

- Easy to transfer ownership.

- Possible tax advantages.

- Easier to raise finance/capital.

Incorporated Company Disadvantages

- Can be expensive to establish, maintain and close down.

- Strict and complex reporting requirements, which can be expensive.

- Separate tax returns for the company and the individual shareholders add expense.

- Need to follow strict legal requirements and comply with Corporations Law.

As I have mentioned, many startup businesses choose sole trader because of the simplicity and low cost. As always, it is best to check with your accountant and/or lawyer with regards what will work best for your personal circumstances.

UNITED STATES

In the US, it's necessary to take into account both legal and tax considerations when selecting a business structure. Which business structure you choose determines which income tax return form you need to file.

The most common structures available are:

- Sole proprietorship

- Partnership

- C corporation

- S corporation

- Limited Liability Corporation (LLC)

Choosing the right structure is important and understanding why that particular structure is right for you is equally important.

Sole Proprietorship

This is the most common business structure. If you are operating your business as a solo operator, or your business is part-time or based on a hobby or personal interest, then sole proprietorship is the simplest business structure.

The structure is inexpensive to set up because there are few legal and tax formalities. If you operate your business as a sole proprietorship, you trade on your own and control and manage the business. You are legally responsible for all aspects of the business – debts and losses cannot be shared.

All the income received and expenses incurred are included on your personal income tax return, your Form 1040 (available on www.irs.gov).

You would also complete a Schedule C (Form 1040) or a Schedule C-EZ (Form 1040). Schedule C helps you calculate the profit, or loss, in your business and the amount, which is called the 'bottom line amount', on the form is transferred to your personal tax return. You need to keep detailed records of expenses and all income earned.

You also need to complete a Schedule SE, which stands for self-employment, along with your Form 1040. This calculates how much self-employment tax you owe. The estimated taxes owed are then paid in four equal amounts throughout the year. With a sole proprietorship, your business earnings are taxed only once. Of course, you will need to check with your accountant to ensure you are paying the correct amount of tax.

Partnership

When it comes to entering into a partnership structure in the US, the same considerations are a factor as in Australia – please refer to the above section.

Sole proprietorship and partnership are unincorporated options. Incorporated options involve shares and shareholders. There is more paperwork involved in the set up and when it comes to ongoing tax returns and other legal filing requirements. An advantage, however, can include limited liability, which generally means creating 'arms-length' distance between the business and the personal assets of the shareholders.

C Corporation

To form a corporation, prospective shareholders provide money, property or both in exchange for capital stock in the corporation. When it comes to calculating taxable income, the deductions that apply to a corporation are generally similar to the sole proprietorship. A corporation can also take special deductions, for example, regarding local and sales taxes paid.

For federal income tax purposes, a C corporation is recognised as a separate tax-paying entity. A corporation conducts business, realises net income or loss, pays taxes and distributes profits to shareholders.

If the corporation makes a profit, the corporation pays tax as and when the profit is earned. The profit is taxed again when it is distributed to shareholders as dividends. This creates a double tax. There is no tax deduction when a corporation distributes dividends to shareholders. Shareholders cannot deduct any loss of the corporation.

S Corporation

An S corporation is a way to avoid double taxation on the corporate income that is associated with a C corp. The corporate income, losses, deductions and credits are passed through to their shareholders for federal tax purposes. Shareholders of S corporations report the flow-through of income and losses on their personal tax returns and are assessed tax at their individual income tax rates.

Limited Liability Company (LLC)

LLC is a business structure allowed by state statute. It is regulated by local jurisdiction. There are a few ways that an LLC may offer greater flexibility for your business. Check with your local state for the regulations. Most states do not restrict ownership of the LLC, which means it can be owned by a range of legal entities, and in most cases, there is no maximum number of members/owners.

Another point of flexibility is that most states allow 'single-member' LLCs, which means that there can be just one owner. The IRS treats one-member LLCs as sole proprietorships for tax purposes. This means that the LLC itself does not pay taxes and does not have to file a return with the IRS. A sole owner of an LLC must report all profits (or losses) of the LLC on Schedule C and submit it with their 1040 tax return.

There are two other important matters for US businesses to address:

1. **Employer Identification Number (EIN).** The EIN is used to identify a business entity and is used to track all the financial transactions of a business. Individuals have social security numbers and a business has an EIN. The EIN is recorded on every business invoice and tax return. You can apply online on the IRS website.

    It doesn't take that long to complete the application online – most people complete it in ten to fifteen minutes – and you usually receive the number immediately. You can only apply, however, during the IRS's hours of operation. (https://www.irs.gov/businesses/small-businesses-self-employed/apply-for-an-employer-identification-number-ein-online).

2. **Sales tax.** Sales tax is state-driven, which means that each state has its own rules about which products and services attract sales tax and what amount of sales tax is to be collected. And these laws are constantly changing. Most states have a destination-based philosophy for collecting sales tax. This means that the sales tax is applicable when the product is used. Origin-based states require the merchant charges the sales tax at the point where the transaction takes place, usually the location of the merchant.

While researching for this book and my online program 'So You Want to Start a Pilates Business', I had a discussion with a sales tax specialist, Mark Best, regarding Pilates businesses. He highlighted for me the big differences you can see in laws by referring to the 'yoga exemption' and the great yoga sales tax wars that took place in 2012. The result of these was yoga not officially being considered exercise for sales tax purposes in New York City. Sales tax really is a matter for the experts, so contact an accountant with sales tax expertise.

Activity for You: Business Structure

As I said at the start of this segment: begin with the end in mind.

Look at the descriptions of each of the business structures and consider the pros and cons of each to decide which structure will work best for you. Remember to consult your lawyer/attorney and/or accountant.

Ultimately, the decision is yours to make in conjunction with your legal advisers. It's worth spending a bit of time on this, however, in order to best set yourself up for success.

Next, we'll turn to some other considerations – how risky is all of this?

RISK MANAGEMENT AND INSURANCES

Starting a business is a risk in itself, and as you grow your business, you will continue to take risks. Risk management is all about taking steps to reduce or avoid the adverse effects. This is where we consider all the things that could go wrong and what to do about them.

It's quite a straightforward process:

- Identify all the things that could go wrong in your business.

- Calculate the likelihood of them happening.

- Develop processes and systems to prevent things going wrong in the first place.

- Identify ways to limit the impact on your business when things do go wrong.

- Ensure the same things don't happen again.

In general, running out of some essential for your business is going to cause a problem. It's important to consider the two key aspects:

- How do you prevent it from happening?

- What do you do if it happens?

Let's look at a couple of examples.

A café could potentially run out of milk. Obviously, that's not great.

- How could they prevent it from happening? They could have a system where the correct amount of milk required for each day is estimated, ordered and delivered.

- How do they limit the impact if it happens? They take cash from petty cash and buy milk from a nearby supermarket, or similar.

A hair salon employs five hairdressers and one calls in sick:

- This is difficult to prevent from happening – people get sick. But having great working conditions can mean you don't suffer as much from people 'pulling sickies'.

- What do you do if it happens? Have a system for contacting clients. Either reschedule them another appointment with the same hairdresser or find them an appointment with another hairdresser.

Most of risk management is really common sense. The thing with common sense is that it usually exists in greater proportion when everyone is calm. It seems to evaporate when things are not going very well.

That's why it is good to have clear systems and processes for what to do if or when things go wrong. Trust me, things *will* go wrong, and you will stand a better chance of riding it out if you've thought through what to do – when everyone is calm!

Insurance is one way of limiting the impact on your business when something goes wrong.

I interviewed Laura Moore for my podcast 'So You Want to Start a Business'. She had a personal fitness business that was located above a fast food shop and one Friday night, the cooking oil caught fire and her studio was destroyed.

Laura talks about how grateful she is that she had insurance. She admits she could have had more, though. How much is enough?

There are a number of different types of insurance that could apply to your business depending on what your business is. Having insurance is optional and not required by law. However, it is highly recommended that you consider the importance of various insurances. If you sign a commercial lease, you may be required by the landlord to have property insurance. Entering into some contracts may have certain insurance policies as a prerequisite for doing business.

Here are some of the insurances you may come across in the course of business:

LIABILITY INSURANCE

This is one of the most important insurance covers because it provides protection if you are found to be legally responsible for personal injury to another person or to their property.

PRODUCT LIABILITY INSURANCE

This specifically covers any products sold or supplied through your business. It provides protection against claims of personal injury or property damage caused by any products sold or supplied through your business.

PROPERTY INSURANCE

This covers damage to property through fire, storm, accident and theft, and covers equipment, signage, furniture, computers and so on.

WORKERS' COMPENSATION INSURANCE

This is compulsory in Australia for all people who are employees of a business. Workers' compensation insurance covers employees who may be injured or become sick in the course of their work; it helps them cover any medical expenses, rehabilitation costs and loss of earnings.

BUSINESS INTERRUPTION INSURANCE

This compensates a business for lost income in the event of a disaster or catastrophic event. This is particularly helpful in paying staff costs, rent expense and the like when the business is unable to trade as normal.

KEY PERSON INSURANCE

This is life insurance for a key person in the business. This would be the owner or a key employee who is super critical to the ongoing success of the business.

MOTOR VEHICLE INSURANCE

This would apply if you use your car for business or have dedicated vehicles.

HOME-BASED BUSINESS INSURANCE

In general, the regular householder's insurance does not cover the business being operated from home. It's possible to request that your insurer include additional cover to cover your business equipment, inventory and so on.

All of the above mentioned insurances attract a premium. The greater the cover, the greater the price of the premium. Insurance premiums would usually be considered a business expense

You may consider whether you want to have forms of personal insurance as well, such as life insurance and health insurance. They are not generally tax deductable expenses, but you can check with your accountant.

Ultimately, how much insurance you want to pay for in your business is your decision. As you might expect, the insurance sales people will try to sell you as much as possible.

This is why it is important to start by identifying all the potential risks in your business and the likelihood of them happening. Then figure out how to prevent them from happening and also what to do if they do happen. Based on this, you can then choose the appropriate levels of insurance.

Activity for You: Developing a Risk Management Plan

Step 1 is to make a list of all the risks – all the things that could go wrong in your business. For example: crashing your computer, losing your laptop, losing a major client, change of government, new competitors entering the market, running out of cash, suppliers not supplying – the list goes on. You can be as specific as necessary, e.g. 'losing laptop that contains all the client contact details and a certain amount of sensitive data.'

Step 2 is to look at each item on the list and determine the probability of that happening. You could use ratings of Low, Medium and High to assess each potential risk.

Step 3 is then to determine the severity of the impact on your business. Again, you could use ratings of Low, Medium and High, or perhaps a number system where 1 is low and 10 is high.

Step 4 is to identify what you would do to minimise the risk from happening or, in fact, remove the risk completely. For some of the items on your list, an insurance policy may well be part of the plan to minimise the impact to the business.

There is a Risk Management Plan Matrix you can download at: http://www.healthynumbers.com.au/book-templates

There aren't many things more important than addressing the risks you're faced with when you own a business.

Next, we're going to turn to another key issue – compliance.

COMPLIANCE MATTERS

Years ago, I worked with a terrific woman. Her name was Norah and she was a workplace health and safety person. We were working together on a project at Qantas. We used to go to these meetings at Brisbane airport and she would say to them, 'You're all going to jail if you don't ...' And then she would tell them what they could potentially go to jail for. For an airline, there are multiple compliance matters, especially around workplace health and safety.

No one wants to go to jail.

The best way to keep your business on the right side of legal compliance is to ensure that you know what the rules are and follow them. Compliance will depend on the nature of your business.

Some of the basic compliance will include:

- Registering with the Tax Office for an ABN or ACN, or the equivalent in your country.

- If you are an incorporated company, adhering to the ASIC, or the equivalent in your country.

- If you register a business name, compliance with business name laws.

- Keeping accurate and up-to-date financial records explaining a company's financial performance. (This is good practice if you're a sole trader, too. It's not just companies that can get audited.)

If you hire employees:

- Adhering to mandatory minimum conditions.

- Paying them the appropriate awards and keeping records.

- Providing a safe and healthy work environment.

- Workers compensation.

If you are preparing food, adhere to the food safety guidelines. If you are in retail, comply with the trading restrictions for certain days and certain hours.

Privacy legislation now requires *all* Australian websites to post a Privacy Policy statement if they collect any personal information. Personal information is information from which a person can be identified.

Meanwhile, business licences, permits and registrations will vary across states and within local councils. It's always best to check with your local authorities what your requirements are.

The businesses that I work with all express a strong desire to be squeaky clean. Ultimately, if you are in any doubt about what is required of you, contact a lawyer for advice.

There's no getting around it, though – when it comes to compliance as well as operations, established systems and processes help.

THE IMPORTANCE OF ESTABLISHING SYSTEMS AND PROCESSES

I'm an unashamed Process Queen. I love to have clear systems for everything in my business and I encourage you to create standardised processes in yours.

What do I mean when I talk about systems and processes?

- A system helps you run your business; for example, a marketing or accounting system. The systems in your business will improve your effectiveness.

- A process is a set of steps to follow to create the same outcome every time. For example, in your café, you make coffee using the same process every time. The processes in your business will improve your efficiency.

Wait. Stay with me, please. I know that some of you reading this are already thinking, 'I want to start my own business because I want to have creative freedom. I want to do things my way.' And I absolutely agree. The processes will be your processes. The systems will be yours. But you still need to create them.

The number one reason is consistency. We want consistency in business so that our clients can experience the greatest possible client experience. When your client first comes to you and when they return to you, they want to know that the way you did what you did yesterday will be the same as what you do today and tomorrow. The only way you can do this is with processes and systems.

Still not convinced? There are other reasons for systems and processes:

- It's easier to outsource or delegate routine tasks.

- You can take holidays and someone else can do what you do.

- It reduces waste – time, materials, effort, money.

- It's easier to train new team members.

- It can help identify problem areas or bottlenecks.

- It creates a base for future improvements.

Let's have a look at a couple of examples. An effective business system is the way you ensure that your clients receive the same experience every time. I've mentioned previously the café where I regularly eat breakfast. They have a clear food and drink ordering and delivery system that guarantees customers get what they order. It comprises a few elements:

1. The customer orders their food and drinks at the cash register, pays the full amount and receives a table number which they take and display on their chosen table.

2. When the order is placed, the cash register system generates drinks orders for the barista. He always makes the coffees and teas in the order the orders are taken. He has no favourites! There is no jumping the queue. Juices are made by one of the kitchen people.

3. The cash register system also generates food orders for the kitchen. The chefs make the food as the orders come in.

4. There is a bell that rings when food or drinks are ready and someone is tasked to deliver them to the customer at their table.

5. People waiting for takeaways hover at the front of the café and the barista calls out when their drinks are ready.

As you can see, this is a relatively simple system to design. Also, each element of the system has sub-systems: the cash register system, the coffee making system, food preparation and so on. Further 'back office' sub-systems would include food ordering and storage.

In many businesses, these systems are informal and are passed from employee to employee. I always suggest that it is a good idea to formalise systems so that when a key person is not there, anyone can figure out what needs to be done. The same applies to processes; it is good business discipline to document your processes.

A Standard Operating Process, or SOP, is a record of the step-by-step activities required to create an outcome. I document my processes for two main reasons:

1. If I am doing a task, it may be a while since I last did it, so I need to be reminded of all the steps so as not to miss any.

2. I can outsource tasks to someone else and know they will give my clients the same experience every time.

Let's look at an example of a process for a hairdresser: taking payment and booking future appointments. There are a number of key aspects to recording this process:

The name: 'Taking payment from client and rebooking future appointments.' If I were working there, I could easily find this and know what it was for.

Date and version number: This helps identify the most up-to-date version of the process.

Aim of the process: This articulates why we are doing this activity. It's important to understand the context of why something needs to be done in a particular way.

Importance of the process: In some businesses, a process may be life critical, e.g. medical sterilisation or maintenance of equipment. Flagging the importance of a process indicates whether it should be prioritised over other processes should there be a resource shortage, for example.

References: This SOP refers to other documented instructions for using the calendar system and the payment system, both of which are necessary to this process. There may not always be a reference.

The actual steps: In some cases, these may need to be extremely detailed, with step-by-step instructions in each of the steps themselves.

The thing about a process like this is that it documents the tactile steps. This still allows for the personality and the individuality of the person following the SOP to flourish as they interact with the client. The following figure illustrates a SOP.

Standard Operating Process: Payment and Rebooking

Procedure Name: Taking payment from client and rebooking their
future appointments

Date updated: 11 April   Version: V1.1

Aim of process:
Ensure all clients:
1. pay in full at the time of consultation
2. are offered additional products for home care of their hair
3. leave with at least their next 2 appointments at times that are convenient to them

Importance of process:
Important to be paid in full. Important for clients to have future appointments to ensure their hair stay looking good and they can have appointments that are times that suit them

References and Resources:
Internet needs to be connected. Instructions for payment gateway. Instructions for using the booking system

Steps:
1. Connect to payment gateway at start of business day
2. Log in to booking system
3. when the client competes their appointment, check if they need any other products to take home with them – conditioner, colour save etc
4. Book future appointments – the 2 if possible.
5. Write appointments on a card or check they have added to their calendar
6. Check system for payment amount for todays consultation
7. Process payment for any products purchased
8. Take total payment using the payment gateway – check it is "approved"
9. Offer receipt to client

Of course at all times we are being friendly, chatty and giving clients the best customer service.

Ultimately, it is a major competitive advantage to have clear systems and processes in your business. It is also an advantage to have a team.

THE POWER OF A SUPPORT TEAM

You truly cannot do it all on your own. You may well be able to do most things, but the reality is that no business is an island. Even if you think you're going it alone, you're surrounded by others you have to engage with.

Ask yourself: who is on your support team? The following outlines a few team members you may be aware of and some of the things to think about when it comes to each group.

THE SUPPORTERS, NO MATTER WHAT

These are the people who always encourage you and support you. Maybe they're friends and family. They will buy your products even if they don't really need or want them. They'll tell their friends about your business. They'll post on your Facebook and Instagram pages, even if they don't quite understand what is going on. Maybe this is your mum? Or your partner? Or your best friend? You do sometimes need to take the enthusiasm of this group with a grain of salt. They love you and want you to be successful, so may protect you from some of the truths that you need to hear.

THE NAYSAYERS

This group of people can add great value to your business as long as you are able to distance yourself from their feedback. They can give you some great perspective on your business. However, watch out for the destructive ones who just want to tear you down. These people are the opposite of the supporters so, again, it's important to take what they say with a grain of salt.

For example, you wish your brother would just tell you that your business idea is great and that it will work. All he seems to come up with are reasons for you not to go into business. 'Have you thought about what will happen if your landlord puts up the rent?' he asks, and you think to yourself, 'Could you just try and be supportive?'

However, your brother may well have just asked a great question – could you manage if the landlord *did* put up your rent?

All feedback is important. You need to be able to take the feedback on board and make it useful, while not taking it personally.

THE REALISTS

This is an invaluable group of people. They may be friends or people in networking groups who have their heads firmly on their shoulders. They aren't overly emotional about your business, and are able to analyse what you're doing dispassionately. They offer the best kind of feedback! If they have started their own business, they will be able to offer you useful insights – listen to them and ask them questions.

SUCCESSFUL BUSINESS PEOPLE, ENTREPRENEURS AND MENTORS

You have to find these people, whether in person or online. Follow them and read their wisdom. Listen to their TED talks. You'll find them everywhere on the Internet. You'll also find them at networking events, chamber of commerce meetings and other business-related activities.

EMPLOYEES

You may need to hire employees. Develop and follow a process for finding and hiring the best people who will fit with your business values and culture.

CONTRACTORS

Your business may not be of a size to support employees and your needs may be sporadic and short-term, so contractors may be a viable option. You can hire locally and have people physically in your business or you may find hiring virtual contractors works for you, based either in your own country or overseas. Create clear contracts. Make expectations explicit so that all parties know and agree to what is expected.

SUPPLIERS

These are the people who will provide the materials, the goods and the equipment you need in your business. Create clear contracts. Make expectations explicit so that all parties know and agree to what is expected.

PARTNERS

What I mean here is not the formal partnership agreements we looked at when we discussed business structure but, rather, people you partner with in the course of running your business. This could include your accountant, your lawyer and your business coach or mentor.

Over time, you will identify various parties with whom to create relationships where you help each other out. This could be formal agreements or more casual arrangements. For example, you might be selling cushions and lamps at the local craft market. You meet someone who sells bespoke candles and you decide to take a stall together for a particular month because offering your products together may enhance the attractiveness to your potential customers. A more complex proposition might involve an ongoing arrangement with financial implications. Even if you're on equal footing, however, create clear contracts. Make expectations explicit so that all parties know and agree to what is expected.

COMMUNITY

What is your relationship with your community? By community, you might think about your physical, local community, your business community, and beyond to the wider community. Community, of course, is now as much online as it is offline. As I have mentioned previously, joining and being part of online communities can certainly attract clients. However, I do encourage my clients not to forget about their offline community, their physical community. Depending on your business, your local community might be where many of your ideal clients are. When they see you active and engaging with the local community, it can increase their desire to be your customer.

As you can see, even if it is just you in the business, there will be many people around you. And it's important to remember that you get to choose whom you surround yourself with and work with. You wouldn't purely want to be surrounded by naysayers, so if you look around at your existing 'support' team and it's made up of ninety per cent negative people, you need to change it up!

Jim Rohn said, 'You're the average of the five people you spend most of your time with.' Whether we like it or not, most of us are greatly influenced by those closest to us. It affects how we think, our self-esteem and the decisions we make. Of course, everyone is their own person, but the research shows that environment has a greater impact on behaviour than many would like to think it does.

I've met a lot of businesspeople who prefer to be the smartest person in the room. Honestly, though, if someone is always ensuring they're the smartest person around, they're hindering their success. In order to learn, we need to be finding and hanging out with people who are actually smarter than we are. That way, we can learn from what they do.

When we surround ourselves with people who are smarter and inspire us, we strive to improve ourselves. Hanging out with negative, lazy or angry people will only make it that much more difficult to stay focussed on building your business. If you have some of these people in your life, it might be time to reduce your involvement with them, otherwise it will hinder your energy, vision and ultimate success.

Activity: Support Team

Think about the five people with whom you spend most of your time. Maybe some of you will have virtual people as well as physical people on your list. One of my people is a podcast. I listen to it a few times a week and I feel I have a relationship with the host. They certainly impact how I feel about myself.

Write down their names.

Assign a numerical value to each person from 1 to 10 – with 10 being the most positive influence possible and 1 the opposite. You might want to think about how they inspire you, how they make you feel, how successful they are in their lives.

Calculate your average.

Look at each individual score and consider how each person affects your average. Perhaps, when you see the results, you'll want to make some changes.

I'm certainly not telling you to get rid of your friends. This activity is just to help you think about the impact of the people you spend the most time with. And if there are some people you feel drag you down emotionally or energetically, it's worth thinking about how to reduce their impact.

This is why reading biographies, for example Elon Musk's or Steve Jobs', is important. Listening to podcasts is important. You're aiming to find people to spend time with who help make you a better business person. They should elevate both your thinking and your performance.

Speaking of performance, now it's time to look at your business finances.

6. YOUR FINANCES

'Being rich is a good thing. Not just in the obvious sense of benefitting you and your family, but in the broader sense. Profits are not a zero sum game. The more you make, the more of a financial impact you can have.'

MARK CUBAN

We know that people start their own business for a variety of different reasons: freedom, flexibility, to make a difference. However, as we've said elsewhere in this book, being in business is also about making money. There are some who want to make a lot of money and others who are aiming to make enough money to live a comfortable lifestyle. Regardless, knowing what's happening with the finances is equally as important as making beautiful products or providing your clients with great service.

Some people just love the finances while others want to turn a blind eye or run for the hills. It's worth keeping in mind that the latter don't create successful startups!

The number one reason that most businesses fail is because they run out of money. Running out of money can literally mean running out of actual cash, or it can mean not having enough in the bank to pay your upcoming obligations. It can mean not making payroll, and not being able to pay your staff this week, or not being able to pay suppliers. Running out of money can also refer to that condition where you don't have enough money to take advantage of a growth opportunity.

Just scraping by is no way to run a business because it can leave you exhausted all the time, trying to figure out where the next amount of money will come from. And getting your finances right is more than managing cash flow – although that is extremely important.

In this chapter, we'll look at the aspects that all new business startups need to pay attention to in order to get their business finances right. When you have your business finances in order, you will be paid the price that is right for what you sell and you will be paid on time. You won't overspend on things that are not important for running your business. And you'll stay inside the rules and regulations as set out in business and tax requirements.

We will now look at a number of simple things that you can do to make it easier to keep your finances on track and make your business a successful one.

BUSINESS STARTUP COSTS

When you first start out in business, there will be a range of one-off costs that relate specifically to getting started and are different to the ongoing running costs and expenses.

Knowing the sorts of general startup costs involved, you can then research to find out what the actual dollar amounts would be for your chosen business. The sorts of costs will be similar; it will the amounts of money involved that will be different across certain businesses.

When you know how much is involved, you can then think about where that money will come from.

The sorts of costs to consider include (and aren't limited to):

Marketing and Advertising

- Website

- Logo design

- Branding

- Signage

- Advertising

- Domain registration

- Website hosting set-up costs

Professional Service Consulting Fees

- Accountant

- Lawyer

- Architect/builder – if necessary

- Business coach

Compliance and Establishment Costs

- Business registration

- ASIC fees

- Licence fees

- Insurance: public liability, professional indemnity, building, contents, business, income, workers

- Council permits

Equipment and Inventory

- Machines

- Tools

- Vehicle

- Office furniture

- Computer

- Software

- Printer

- Shop front equipment: cash register, refrigerators

- Starting inventory

Printing and Stationery

- Signage

- Business cards

- Flyers, posters

- Brochures

Occupancy Costs

- Fit out

- Fixtures

- 'Make good' costs at the end of the lease

- Full clean at start and end of lease

- Rental bond – can be up to six months

- Connecting Internet

- Electricity, water and other services, including deposits and connection fees

If you are starting out as a hairdresser, you can imagine there are specific costs for fitting out a salon, including chairs, plumbing and so on. A flower shop would require a fit out with fridges, benches, storage and display areas. Each business will have it's own specific startup costs as well as the costs which apply to every business.

People often ask me how much they should allow for startup costs. There really is no one answer. Each business needs to make their list of potential startup costs and do the research.

The more effort you put into finding out the actual costs involved, the more accurate your total costs are likely to be. You could call providers and get quotes for things like logo design and website. If you are considering leasing premises, you can research rental costs online. You'll start to get a sense that there is a range – you can do things more cheaply at one end of the spectrum, right up to the other end of the spectrum where you can spend a lot of money getting your business up and running. In fact, the sky is pretty much the limit.

I usually suggest to my clients that they start with a wish list. Then, they can always prioritise the essentials above the 'nice to haves'. For example, having a website is pretty much essential. Clients like to be able to see that you exist, and having a website, even a really basic site, is preferred to not having one at all. (A Home page and About You page are the two most important things to have if you are going super basic. Plus a Contact Us page.)

Activity: Startup Costs

Think about what's important for your business. Use the checklist above for inspiration and make a list of all your likely startup costs. Do your research to calculate how much your list will cost you. If the total seems very high, prioritise the different categories and identify what's essential, and what you might be able to leave until later.

FUNDING YOUR STARTUP

Once you know how much you need, the next thing to consider is where the money will come from. The decisions you make now about how to fund your business may have longer term implications. If you take the cautious approach and save for your startup, you may miss the opportunity. On the other hand, if you are super keen to get started and over borrow and then things don't work out, you could face financial ruin – like so many business startups in the past.

When it comes to the startup costs, there are a couple of ways that you could find the funds:

JOB INCOME

If you are starting off part-time in your business and still working in a full-time job for another business, then your income from your job could be the main source of funds for getting started. You can use your own money to pay for the things you need to set up. This is a very common model for paying startup costs.

SELLING PERSONAL BELONGINGS

You could sell things that you are no longer using on eBay or Gumtree or hold a garage sale. I have a client who funded her entire business startup through selling off all the things she didn't need. She said to me during one of our early coaching calls: 'You know, Ingrid, I'm going to be so busy for the next two years, I won't have time for all these things, and by the time I'm ready to use them all again, they'll all be out of date or out of fashion.'

Another word of warning here: don't get so caught up having a great time selling things on eBay that you forget about your business.

PRESELLING BUSINESS PRODUCTS OR SERVICES

You may be able to presell your products or services. For example: a one-year membership paid up-front could attract a certain percentage discount. If you are offering this to clients predisposed to know, like and trust you, this can be a great way to inject funds into your business at the start, as well as any other time when you need to raise funds.

The options above are examples of bootstrapping. This is where you fund your business completely by yourself. A famous example is MailChimp, an online e-newsletter provider that has been completely bootstrapped. They have never sought funding, investors or capital injections from anyone other than the people who own and run the business. This may seem incredibly attractive, but it might not always be possible, so it's worth considering your options. Sometimes a combination of approaches may be the answer.

FRIENDS AND FAMILY

You could ask for investment from friends and family. They may invest directly, or loan the money for a period of time to help you get established.

A word of warning about friends and family. I had a client some time ago who set up an acupuncture clinic and she borrowed money from her brother. Because he had lent her the money, he thought it gave him the right to have a say in how she ran her acupuncture clinic. She arranged to have a loan from the bank to pay back the money to her brother and that stopped him interfering.

My second tip in regards to friends and family is that, like any other legal arrangement in your business, it is wise to have a written document that clearly articulates the terms and conditions of the loan – signed by all parties.

CREDIT

You could use your credit card, though this is not the best option. I would always think of this as an absolute last resort due to high interest rates charges on outstanding balances. However, if you need something that is going to win a client or some work, and you know you'll be able to pay your card off quickly before any large interest charges, then it's smart to use credit to grow your business.

BANK LOAN

Many of the banks are keen to support small businesses, so you may be able to negotiate a special interest rate. Again, you just need to be sure the business will be able to afford the loan payments and the interest.

MICRO LOAN

These are slightly different to bank loans in that they involve a smaller amount for a shorter period of time. A number of micro loan specialists have started offering these types of loans. Again, always check the details and contracts, and make sure that you will have the financial capacity in your business to repay the loan.

GRANTS FROM THE GOVERNMENT OR OTHER AGENCIES

Applying for grants can be extremely time-consuming so, again, keep your focus on running your business. What will be the value of the grant compared to the amount of time and effort required to complete and submit the application? If the amount of the grant far outweighs the value of your time and effort, then this could be a good option. Depending on the likelihood of your success of receiving a grant, it may be worthwhile contracting a grants application specialist to submit your application.

INCUBATOR

In the last few years, business incubators have been popping up and offering support to startups. A business incubator is a company that provides a range of services to help new and startup businesses. The concept of incubators started in the late 1950s in the US and has become increasingly common in recent years as more people start businesses. Because business startups lack necessary resources, experience and networks, incubators can be invaluable getting them through the initial hurdles. These hurdles include space, funding, legal concerns, accounting requirements, computer services and other prerequisites to running the business. Acceptance into an incubator program is mostly by application. If you get involved in an incubator program, check the terms and conditions very clearly. Some of them stipulate that the incubator owns a percentage of your business.

CROWDFUNDING

There are some terrific examples of wildly successful startups using this form of fundraising. The idea of crowdfunding or crowdsourcing is that a business offers a product, or service, for sale prior to it being available. The money raised is then used to produce and ship the product. I personally supported a crowdfunding campaign for a stand-up desk. I had met the inventor/developer and believed that it would be a good investment. I paid for the desk in advance and it was shipped when completed. I also personally invested in a book that was being written. This was quite a different example to the desk because there were a variety of options for investment, all at different price points. The e-book was the most basic option. The top option was a day with the author and multiple copies of the physical book.

A word of caution about using this method of funding. It can be wildly successful or a dismal failure. It is not just a case of setting it up and watching the money roll in. There is significant work required pre-launch, and getting attention is vital to success. That said, it's a great way to ascertain whether there really is a market for your idea. Maybe the cucumber guy (see page 57) could have tried this option.

There are two things that I personally believe about funding a business startup:

- If you are prepared to put in a significant portion of your own money, this impacts your level of commitment, often referred to as 'skin in the game'.

- Asking your customers to fund your business indicates whether your product or service is truly viable; that is, whether it 'has legs'. If customers are prepared to fund your business, it demonstrates a significant level of commitment from them and gives a strong indication of demand in the marketplace.

You certainly wouldn't want to miss an opportunity due to a lack of financial resources but, at the same time, you don't want to run the chance of losing everything. So, as always, seek professional advice before you make any significant decisions regarding funding for your business.

YOUR BREAK-EVEN POINT

While the break-even point is an accounting term, it is one that we all need to understand for our business. In simple terms, it is the point at which the cost to create your product or service is fully met by the amount you receive for it – that's why it's called 'breaking even'. There is no profit, but also no loss. A business needs to know it's break-even point in order to set prices that get them there in a set timeframe.

Basically, there are two types of costs in a business – fixed and variable. The variable costs are the costs involved in actually creating the product. They vary with how many products you make.

For example, a business makes and sells a simple table – the table has a top and four legs. If you make one table, let's say the costs are $50 and if you make ten tables, the costs are 10 x $50 = $500. The costs vary along with your production.

We know we can sell a table for $125 and the costs are $50. $125 less $50 and it appears we make $75 profit on every table. Wow! That looks terrific! This amount is referred to as the contribution margin.

However, the variable material costs are just part of the costs involved in producing and ultimately selling the table. We also need to consider the fixed costs involved in the business – these are required to actually run the business. They are called fixed costs despite the fact they may fluctuate a bit, month to month. They remain fixed irrespective of how much business you do. Examples of fixed costs are rent, monthly phone expense, wages (including yours), interest payments, Internet, insurance and accounting fees.

Let's say that in one month, the total costs to run the business add up to $2,500.

In order to establish the break-even point for this simple table-making business, we need to ask: how many tables do we need to sell a month, with a profit of $75 per table, in order to cover the total fixed costs of $2,500?

This is a really useful piece of information because we now we know that when we sell 33.3 tables – let's say thirty-four tables – in a month, then the business breaks even. What this means is that at the break-even point of thirty-four tables, there is enough money coming in to cover all the outgoings.

What we also know is that for every table sold beyond thirty-four, each $75 made is pure profit.

What else does this tell us? It tells us how many tables we need to sell every day that we operate.

If there are thirty or thirty-one days in a month and we are selling tables every day of the month, then this equates to slightly more than one table every day. 34/31 = 1.1 tables every day (1.2 tables in February). You get the idea. If the business only works five days a week, then it is closer to two tables per day. 34/20 = 1.67. Knowing this information is extremely powerful.

Calculating the break-even point for every business is a variation of this calculation. Can you imagine trying to calculate break-even in one of the large supermarkets? They have very large spreadsheets. In fact, they have extremely sophisticated calculations and algorithms.

Some people get excited when they calculate a deceptively large contribution margin on their product. For example, I have heard people looking at starting a café say, 'I sell a cup of coffee for $4 and it only costs 26 cents to make every cup.' This can look like a huge contribution margin of $3.74 per cup of coffee. The reality is that this only takes into account the coffee part. What about the cost of the paper cup? The takeaway trays, sugar? What about the milk? Cashew milk, almond milk, soy? When you take these into account, the contribution margin shrinks considerably.

If I were working with a café owner, I might ask, 'How much rent are you going to pay? In fact, how much are your total fixed costs? Let's look at the true cost of each cup of coffee and then calculate how many cups of coffee you need to sell each and every day in order to pay your rent and other costs.'

If your business provides a service rather than making and selling a product, this calculation is much simpler. You would calculate the total costs for each month and then charge that amount to clients for the month. In reality, you would probably calculate over the period of a quarter or a year. Your costs might be $20,000 per year and you might want to pay yourself $100,000 to cover your expenses, so your total billings would add up to $120,000 for the year – that would be breaking even. Charge your clients more and you make a profit. Charge less and you make a loss.

A business that is not clear about their break-even amount is operating in the dark. Not knowing how much income the business needs to generate every month, every week, every day can lead to failure. You need to make sufficient funds to continue operating. That's what makes pricing is so important.

PRICING

Now that you have information about your break-even point, you can start to look at the various pricing models available to you. In our basic break-even calculation, we used an arbitrary market price for the table and for a cup of coffee. In this section, we are going to look more closely at the various influences on price. Price setting involves knowing your business, your clients and the market that you are operating in.

Why is it important to get the price right? Set the price too high – without positioning yourself in the market – and you risk making no sales. I find this is less common, though. Business startups have a tendency to price low. But set the prices too low and you won't make money. You won't make profit and, ultimately, your business will fail. Setting prices too low to start with makes it difficult to increase your prices going forward. You can also open yourself up to being perceived as a discount or cheap brand. So how do you go about it?

There are a few different ways to set your prices.

MARK-UP

This is always based on cost and is the difference between the actual cost and the selling price. For example, if we take our table from the previous example: It costs $50 to make the table and it sells for $125. The mark-up is $75 on the actual cost, or 150%:

$$75/50 = 1.5 \text{ x } 100 = 150\%$$

MARGIN

This is always based on the sales price and is the percentage difference between the selling price and the gross profit. So let's use the same example: sales price is

$125 and the cost is $50. The actual profit per table is $75 and the margin is 60 per cent. We calculate this by dividing profit by revenue:

$$75/125 = 0.6 = 60\%$$

VALUE

A great way to think about pricing is in terms of value. Think of some of the electronic equipment we buy. What we pay for is the value. We pay almost $1,000 for a mobile phone, which actually probably only costs a few dollars to physically make. The value is based on what the phone can do for us, what it says about us just by owning one, and what we would miss out on if we didn't have one.

How much value does your customer perceive they are gaining when they pay for your product or service? The more value, the higher the price they will pay.

In some cases, you may need to test what is referred to as 'what the market will bear'.

Why are designer clothes more expensive than off-the-rack items in the supermarket? Is it that they are unique? Their design? Perceived prestige? Limited availability? Just yesterday, my nephew was looking at a picture of a stunning watch. We looked it up online and the first thing he noticed was that there were only 500 of these watches available. 'Wow, Auntie,' he said. 'Imagine owning one of only 500 in the world,' and he's only eight years old!

How you position yourself in the market plays an important part in your pricing strategy. The more someone values what you offer, the more they will be prepared to pay. In fact, the more they value what you offer, the more price becomes irrelevant.

TIERED PRICING MODEL

This is where you have basic, premium and prestige pricing – or bronze, silver and platinum. The lower price gets the client a basic level of service, the next one up gets them a higher level of service, and, therefore, more value, and the top price gets them the best service – providing the best value.

I had a client some years ago who provided IT support. When she first started her business, she was happy to have any clients she could get. Over time, as her reputation grew, she became progressively more busy and employed people to help her provide service and value to her clients. She retained some of her original clients and they were still paying close to the original fees they had started out at. This was a problem for her because she had always provided them great service for that price and when she came to me for help, she knew she couldn't continue to give the same level of value to these long-term clients who were still paying for the old startup process.

This is such a common example of what happens when a business starts off. It can be very tempting to take just anyone to pay the bills. The main reason this becomes a problem is that few businesses have a strategy for how to increase prices as they start to grow and gain reputation in the marketplace.

It's all too easy to end up like this client with too many clients still paying that low startup price and, at the same time, expecting to receive the improving levels of service.

You may be wondering how we solved this? We introduced a tiered pricing model.

We came up with a pricing model that actually reflected what her business had become. As an IT provider, she offered three levels of service, so we created three price levels. Immediate response to any IT issue was the premium service offer and that cost the most. A response within twenty-four hours was the third level and this had the lowest price. A response within three hours was the middle level and this was priced between the two other options. All clients were offered the opportunity to join the level they were prepared to pay for.

What was actually very interesting in this particular case was that many of the people who had been with her the longest opted for the middle or top tier. She'd never asked them to pay more, so they hadn't. They valued her service, however, and were prepared to pay for it. Sometimes, you just need to set up a pricing structure and ask for the payment.

Recurring Pricing Model

This is where you set up so that your clients pay you every month. The previous example included this recurring pricing model as well as the tiered approach. The price they paid was a monthly subscription for their IT support.

Dollar Shave Club is probably one of the best examples of this. Customers pay a fixed dollar amount every month and they receive new blades every month. The gym membership model is the same. You sign up and pay a fixed amount every month, whether you use the gym or not.

Some of you may be thinking about signing up to Xero or MYOB for your bookkeeping software – they both use a recurring pricing model.

Almost every business can find a way to create a recurring pricing model and there are a number of reasons why having this set-up is beneficial to your business:

- It creates even inwards cash flow for the business.

- You know how much you will have coming in every month based on how many clients you have signed up to the recurring model.

- Customers have the convenience of knowing how much they have to pay every month.

- A monthly fee can often be more affordable for clients than an annual fee or upfront payment.

- Setting up a subscription or recurring payment gives your business an advantage over businesses that don't offer a subscription option.

- It's relatively easy to set up and maintain.

Freemium

In Chapter 5, I mentioned WordPress as an option for setting up your website. This is a great example of a pricing model called 'freemium'. This is a business model where the basic version is free of charge. To gain access to more advanced options, you pay. WordPress offers a wide range of themes for websites free of charge. For the more advanced themes and customisation, the company charge.

Another examples of the freemium model is LinkedIn. You can join LinkedIn for free, but for the more advanced options, there is an annual fee. MailChimp is yet another example. The basic version of MailChimp is free, and for that you can send a set number of emails every month to a list with a limited number of names and email addresses. As you come to want more features for your email system, you upgrade to the level you require. Dropbox is the same. You can access the minimum storage for free and then pay more to store more.

Check Out the Competition

I never recommend that you set your prices based on what the competition charge. However, I do strongly recommend that you regularly check what the competition charges for what they offer. It's also a good idea to regularly check any changes to their offering – any additions, bonuses and so on. It's not so you can copy, but so you can stay aware.

Discounts

You may not have considered discounting as a pricing strategy. I include it here because there are businesses that choose to set themselves up as 'discounters'; for example, the discount chemists, the 'we'll beat any price' discount retailers and the discount fashion outlets. Many of the retailers have trained us not to shop at full price because there will be a sale on soon – the 'end of financial year' sale or 'end of season' sale are the main two.

Every business has a place on the spectrum and having a strategy that is all about discounting certainly works for some. Discounts can also be used as a one-off or occasional incentive for customers to make a purchase.

Sometimes, a client will ask me, 'What if I set the price at $200 and then cross it out and say twenty per cent discount – would that make it sound better?' As a customer, are any of us really fooled by this approach? But we do see some businesses offer multiple purchase discounts. 'Buy 1 for $20. Buy 2 for $35 and save $5.' This sort of pricing can work well for socks, candles and consumables

– lower priced items. Your business idea might lend itself to having a discount strategy or to having occasional discount incentives.

Regardless, I always like to remind my clients that when a business offers discounts, it sends a certain message to its clients.

As you can see, there are a number of ways that you can approach a pricing strategy for your business. There is no one right way to set your prices, whether for products or services. You might find that a combination of pricing strategies will work for you.

The one thing that is essential is that the amount of money coming in – that is, your sales revenue – must be more than the total costs in your business. A business cannot sustain more going out than coming in. It also needs to keep on track of its tax obligations, so it knows where it stands.

TAXES

I'm writing this book in Australia where our Australian Taxation Office (ATO) is the principal revenue collection agency of the Australian government. *The role of the ATO is to effectively manage and shape the tax and superannuation systems that support and fund services for Australians.*

Pretty much everywhere in the world will have a similar government body that regulates and manages revenue collection through taxation. It's worth checking the website for your country. I suggest you go to Google and type in the name of your country and 'tax office' to find your government tax collection agency.

There may be small differences to the rate of tax to pay and the items you can and cannot claim as tax deductible. The annual cycle is also likely to be different depending on where you are reading this and considering setting up your business. Every country will have rules about keeping records, declaring your financial records and paying tax on profits.

There are two key reasons why understanding what is expected of you with regards to taxes and financial record keeping is important.

The first is obvious. You want to abide by the rules as set out by your tax office so that you avoid breaking any laws. In the long run, this will keep you out of jail – at the extreme end – and prevent you from having to face prosecution and/or pay fines. In cases where I have known clients to be investigated by the ATO, this is not only damaging to the business and the personal reputation of the people involved, it can also have an impact on the future viability of the business.

Second, you want to pay the correct amount of tax in a timely manner. If your record keeping is sloppy or inaccurate, you may end up paying more tax than necessary. If your financial records are not up to date and you then submit two or three years' of tax returns at the same time, you may have to pay three years of tax all at once, and that will likely have a significant impact on cash flow. I had a client who started working with me last year who had just submitted two years' tax returns together and now faced a large tax bill. Fortunately, in Australia, there is provision to pay off a tax debt over time. He came to me for coaching because he wanted figure out how to pay it off as fast as possible! The interest rates are pretty steep.

It's worth remembering that paying tax is a good thing because it means your business is making a profit. Sometimes, someone in my 'So You Want to Start a Business' classes will ask, 'How do you arrange it so that you don't pay any tax?' One way not to pay any tax is not to make any money! You pay tax when you make a profit in your business. Of course, no one wants to pay more than they have to. That's where having a skilled accountant will help you get the balance right – staying legal and only paying your fair share of tax based on your revenue and all your allowable deductions.

Wherever you are in the world, be aware of what is expected of you from a legal tax compliance perspective and do the right thing. The best way to ensure you are staying on the right side of the laws of your country is to engage a qualified and registered accountant and bookkeeper. You may want to do some of the basics yourself, but consider whether this would be the best use of your time. Having your accounts prepared on a regular basis by a professional will ensure you remain compliant with the tax regulations of your country.

However you choose to do it, there are innumerable business benefits you can gain from having your financials up to date.

KEEPING UP WITH YOUR FINANCIALS

My business is called Healthy Numbers for a reason. As I've written elsewhere, I personally love numbers. They can give you all kinds of information about the health of your business.

In the previous section, we learned that it is important to keep financial records up to date for compliance reasons. You also want your financial records up to date so that you can use the reports to gauge the financial health of your business.

Keeping your records up to date is the first part. Actually reading the reports and paying attention to the information contained in them is equally important.

There are three basic reports to pay attention to:

Profit and loss (P&L): This is a summary of the money coming in and the money going out over a period of time. Profit = more in than out. Loss = more going out than coming in.

Balance sheet: This is a snapshot of the assets and liabilities in your business at a particular point in time.

Cash flow: This is the movement of monies in and out of your business. Forward projection of cash flow is especially critical for businesses where careful management of the timing of cash in and cash out is the difference between the business having sufficient cash to meet its payments. Running out of cash is never a good thing.

In every business, these three financial reports tell you the basics. It is important to pay attention to them on a regular basis. What does regular mean? That will depend on what business you are in. I personally recommend at least monthly, even weekly, if at all possible. I have personally worked in situations where we tracked financial performance on a daily basis. In one manufacturing company I worked with many years ago, we had sophisticated financial software that calculated how much profit the business was making every fifteen minutes! I'm certainly not suggesting any of you will want that level of scrutiny. But I will go so far as to predict that even those of you reading this who say, 'I'm not really into numbers, and no good at maths,' will one day find yourself addicted to the information in your financial reports – especially when it is healthy financial news!

Let's take a closer look at each report.

PROFIT AND LOSS

When your record keeping is up to date, you know at any point in time whether your business is making a profit or is operating at a loss. If you are only doing your accounts quarterly, or worse, annually, things can reach a point where you are not actually making enough money to cover your costs – and you don't even realise it.

Would it not be better to know sooner rather than later so that you can rectify the issue? One of the first things I work on with my clients is to have them understand their financials. I always say, 'You don't have to actually do the accounts yourself,' and I would say the same to you. You do, however, need to be in a position to understand the importance of keeping up-to-date records and understand what the numbers tell you about your business.

Being able to identify if there are financial issues early is extremely important in business. Up-to-date financial records will certainly help with this.

Being able to see just how profitable your business is can be very satisfying. It affirms that your business is running successfully and will continue to do so in the future. Knowing how you are performing financially can help you make decisions about business growth and expansion, about introducing additional products and services, and help you get the timing right when it comes to growing your team.

BALANCE SHEET

Depending on the size of your business, you may have relatively few assets and liabilities, so this could be quite a simple report. In fact, if you are operating in Australia as a sole trader, you don't need to complete a balance sheet for tax compliance at the time of writing this book.

I do recommend keeping track of your balance sheet, however, and this can be simplified using accounting software. Some of the interesting and useful information included is the liability to pay GST, Pay as You Go tax (PAYG) for any employees and superannuation.

Having up-to-date P&L and balance sheets in your business can also draw attention to a range of other important aspects:

- Have all your clients paid you for their goods or their services or are there outstanding amounts?

- How much is outstanding?

If you do not have a system for issuing invoices in a timely manner, you risk losing money by not being paid for work you have competed or products you have supplied. In addition, you can lose time chasing payments from slow paying clients. This takes energy away from doing your good work.

- Are there outstanding monies owed to suppliers?

- Have you paid all your suppliers on time?

Your suppliers will expect to be paid on time and they may withhold supply if they are not paid. Sloppy record keeping can result in bills being missed or not paid when they are due.

- Have you been charged the right amount for all the supplies/items you have bought?

There are numerous ways you can be overcharged in business:

- Paying for items you didn't order.

- Being charged twice for the same items or service.

- Continuing to pay for something you are no longer using.

- Being charged a different price to the agreed price.

- Not being given an agreed discount.

In many instances, the errors can be corrected. The thing is that correcting errors takes time and energy. If you have good record keeping practices in place, then mistakes are less likely to happen.

- Are you making enough profit to consider employing more people?

Any time you think about bringing additional people into your business, there will be additional costs to consider. Your financial reports can help answer the following:

- Is the business making enough money to pay for more people?

- How long will it take for the person's salary to be covered by additional revenue?

- Do you have the funds to introduce new products? Buy new equipment?

Knowing how you are performing financially can help you make decisions about introducing additional products and services, and growing the business.

In the early days, when it is just you running your business, it may be quite straightforward for you to keep track of all the ongoing running costs – both fixed and variable. As your business grows and more people become involved, you will need to find straightforward ways to track the cost of everything in your business.

If you do not set up systems early, costs can get out of control. If you do not have guidelines when new people come into your business, they may not have the same approach as you.

Excessive costs can destroy your business. As we've just mentioned, over-ordering and paying too much for items can place an unnecessary financial burden on anyone. It's much more serious for a startup, which is already challenged to fund everything. There will be times when you get really busy in your business and, unless there are systems in place, your suppliers could increase prices without you noticing. Every time the cost of your supplies increases, that eats into your profitability.

When you look at figures comparatively, you can see the fluctuations. Investigate fluctuations in the report. For example, the P&L report shows a similar amount against an expense, let's say 'bank charges', and it is about $400 every month. Then, suddenly, it is $600 in one month. Ask, 'Why is it different this month?' There is usually a rational explanation: 'We made more sales that month so had more bank charges', or 'We paid for a new account set-up.' It may, however, be an error: 'Oh that $200 should have been for printing costs and was miscoded', or 'It was charged in error and the bank refunded it the following month – see, it's only $200 the following month.'

The best way to ensure that everyone tracks costs and expenses in your business is to create systems, processes and guidelines so that everyone knows what to do.

Both P&L and balance sheet are easily produced by your bookkeeper at the end of every week, month and quarter for your examination. Setting aside time in your schedule to look through your reports is part of being a business owner. If you don't understand what the reports are telling you, then ask your bookkeeper or accountant. You may also find it beneficial to discuss the financial reports with a business coach.

MANAGING CASH FLOW

Cash is King. Having cash flow is vital to business success. I'm not talking about a bag of $100 notes. What cash means is having money in the bank, actual funds available to spend.

The P&L can show the business making profit, yet there may be no money in the bank – no actual funds available for payments. This can be one of the most difficult concepts for the new business owner to grasp.

'I'm making a profit. Why do I have no money?' This is a common question asked by business owners and not just at the startup stage. Running out of money can happen to a business any time. Sometimes, it might not be immediately apparent why there is no cash at a given point in time.

Managing cash flow means projecting the cash position for your business in order to identify if there is a point in time where you will run out of money; that is, not have enough money to pay your obligations. For example, if your rent is due – $4,400 for the month – and you only have $2,000 in the bank, you cannot pay your rent. Or, you need to pay for supplies and the invoice is for $1,000, but you only have $500 in the bank.

If you are monitoring the future cash flow in your business then you will be able to identify the point in time where this might happen and you could take steps to mitigate the business from actually running out of money.

When it comes to managing cash flow, there are two key questions to consider:

- How can a business run out of cash? What are the reasons that cause this to happen?

- What can the business do about it? What are the things a business can do to be and stay cash flow positive?

The simple problem will be more money going out of the business than money coming in. The reasons for this happening are many and varied. A few examples and solutions follow.

STARTUP COSTS

A startup has a number of one-off purchase requirements, for example computers, a website, branding and compliance costs. Many of these are one-off costs that require either pre-payment or payment on completion. Many of these are quite expensive. The reason this can be so damaging to cash flow is that, in the early stages, there may be little income and the burden of paying for startup costs can erode what little income there is.

What Can You Do About It?

We covered this in the section about funding your startup. Make sure you generate sufficient funds to cover all the startup costs:

- Save up or bootstrap the startup costs.

- Sell things on eBay.

- Borrow – from a bank, family or other sources.

- Rent equipment instead of buying.

- Presell your products or services – getting money in from future customers.

LACK OF CREDIT WITH SUPPLIERS

A business startup is asked by suppliers to pay for everything in advance because, as a startup, they have no credit record. For example, when a café or a wine bar starts trading, having no credit rating with the suppliers, everyone demands cash on delivery. If the business has only just stared to trade, there may be low cash reserves with which to handle this.

What Can You Do About It?

- Negotiate with suppliers to pay on account. As the suppliers become more confident that you are a viable business, they will be more comfortable allowing you to do so. Here's a tip: if you are offered to pay on account, then pay on time. There is nothing that will annoy a supplier more than having to chase payments.

- Shorten the purchase cycle. For example, instead of buying a month's worth of supplies, buy weekly. This can reduce the outgoing cash.

Established businesses also experience cash flow issues from time to time. Some of the key reasons are outlined below.

TIMING

You pay your supplier for goods or for stock before your customer pays you for your products or service. This is a business model that naturally causes a negative cash flow.

What Can You Do About It?

- Presell your product or service to your customers and clients.

- Take deposits for future sales.

- Align your payment terms with your sales cycle.

DEBT

The business is paying off large amounts of debt, or even small amounts. Interest payments can cripple a business, especially loans and lease payments structured over a short period of time.

What Can You Do About It?

- Pay off loans as quickly as possible to minimise the interest expense.

- Instead of borrowing money, come up with ways to pay for expansion from the existing business.

NOT CHARGING ENOUGH FOR YOUR PRODUCT OR SERVICE

The actual price charged for the product or service is not enough to cover the cost of producing the product or service. This business will find itself borrowing more and more money just to stay in business. Eventually, you will need to make a decision to charge more or shut the business down.

What Can You Do About It?

Charge more for what you do!

OWNER DRAWINGS

It's easy to take money out of the business to pay yourself and you can end up taking too much.

What Can You Do About It?

Do you remember earlier in the book, I told you about Dermalogica and how the owners paid themselves almost nothing for the first few years they were in business? Sometimes, business owners need to make decision to pay themselves last and keep the money in the business.

Use the financial reports to calculate a realistic amount to pay yourself and leave sufficient funds to run the business.

ORDERING AND HOLDING TOO MUCH STOCK

Many business owners do not pay enough attention to the amount of funds they have tied up in stock at any point in time. For example, a product the business uses is offered on special so they buy in bulk only to find that paying for a year's worth of it causes problems. It puts extreme pressure on cash flow and begs the question: where to store it? I actually had a client who did this. They bought a year's worth of consumables that they used in their business because they saved such a lot of money and then had to pay for storage because they had nowhere to keep it. They underestimated how much space a year's worth of tissues, paper towels and toilet paper could take up.

What Can You Do About It?

Create a list of all the items you need in your business and identify the minimum and maximum stock level for each. Order according to needs, not specials.

NOT ENOUGH SALES

This may seem obvious. There just are not enough sales to cover the costs in the business.

What Can You Do About It?

It is important for the business to know the break-even point; that is, what volume of sales is required to cover all the expenses every week, month or annually. This is the minimum sales required for the business to break even. The sales strategy needs to generate a level of sales to more than break even – to ensure positive cash flow.

There are three ways to increase sales:

1. Encourage more customers to buy from you.

2. Encourage the customers you already have to buy more often.

3. Encourage customers to buy a bigger volume of products or services.

Take, for example, a sandwich shop that has regular customers and wants to increase sales. Using the three ways above, they could:

1. Run a promotion or advertising campaign to encourage new customers to come into the shop.

2. Start a loyalty program that gets customers who maybe come in once a week to visit on more days of the week.

3. Encourage customers to buy more using the famous 'Would you like fries with that?' approach. I was buying a Japanese rice bowl only the other day and, as we were making the selections, they asked me, 'Would you like to add avocado?' I answered, 'Yes,' automatically, which added $3 onto my dish!

FLUCTUATING DEMAND

This refers to fluctuations that may be caused by:

- Seasonality

- Day of the week

- Month of the year

- Weather

- Public holidays and long weekends

- School holidays

What Can You Do About It?

Most fluctuations can be anticipated. Create a plan for how to deal with the fluctuations in sales that affect cash flow.

- If you know there are fewer sales in January, resulting in less cash in the bank, then make sure you have a massive push in the run up to Christmas.

- Run marketing campaigns.

- Plan to save money during the year to have funds for the rainy days.

- Look at your expenses for the month and reduce unnecessary payments.

NOT ISSUING INVOICES

Sometimes a business provides products or services and does not invoice the customer.

I remember being at a networking breakfast and one of the people was giving a glowing recommendation for a local plumber. 'He did a great job and it's been two weeks and I still haven't received an invoice from him; maybe he's forgotten.' If our plumber is really busy and doing all his own bookkeeping and invoicing, he may well have.

This is one of the most surprising reasons I hear for a business not having cash coming in, considering the business environment we are operating in today with all the various types of software available. There is no excuse for not issuing invoices for products or services.

What Can You Do About It?

Have a system to keep track of who has and who has not been issued with invoices for the service provided or the products sold. Sign up for accounting software that automatically issues invoices.

POOR DEBTOR MANAGEMENT

I see this all too often. A business issues an invoice to a customer or client and the invoice remains unpaid despite the product being delivered or the service provided.

What Can You Do About It?

- Have a process to actually take money from the client or customer before or at the time the product is delivered or service provided.

- If the business issues an invoice, have a system to follow up payment for invoices sent and collect that debt.

NEGLECTING TO SET ASIDE MONIES THAT ARE NOT THEIRS

If a business collects GST and leaves it in their 'every day' account, this gives a false sense of cash in the business. This money does not belong to the business – it belongs to the ATO and/or the superannuation funds. When the time comes to pay the GST and the superannuation, the business has spent the monies on operational costs.

What Can You Do About It?

One of the things that I insist on when I am working with clients is that they establish a separate bank account for their GST, PAYG tax, superannuation and income tax. Sanction the funds into a separate account, and there will always be sufficient to pay the obligations when they arise. I also recommend, if the business is operating at a profit, that they sanction appropriate funds to pay the future tax liability.

GROWING TOO QUICKLY

This may seem counterintuitive to some people. It might seem that we want the business to grow and grow quickly. However, fast growth actually puts enormous pressure on cash flow and can result in a business having to borrow funds. This adds further pressure as the debt incurs interest.

What Can You Do About It?

Plan for growth and fund growth from profit.

These are just some of the reasons for negative cash flow and some of the ways you can mitigate against actually running out of money. There are whole books written on this topic.

For a business to be viable in the long term, it must be able to generate positive cash flow continuously. There will be times when there are large outflows of cash due to major purchases or seasonal factors. When the business is managing its cash flow effectively, it is able to ride out the dips with reserves accumulated during the peak times of cash inflow. Serious problems arise when there are more net outflows than net inflows.

So what does a business do to ensure there is sufficient cash flow? The first thing to do is to track and project cash flow. If cash flow is critical, then this would be best tracked every day. Once it is set up in an Excel spreadsheet or using bookkeeping software, it becomes straightforward.

In its very simplest form, the calculation can go as follows:

Cash at bank at today: **$1,000.00**

Date	Add cash in	Less cash out	Net position	Comment
Today	500.00		1,500.00	
Today		450.00	1,050.00	
Tomorrow	0	200.00	850.00	
Next day	0	600.00	250.00	Make phone calls to get cash in
Next day	1,000.00	0	1,250.00	
				Visit extra customers to promote X product to generate more sales
Next week: Rent		2,000.00	−750.00	
And so on				

You can see in this example, the cash went down to $250 and in the comments you see: 'Make phone calls to get cash in.'

You can also see that the rent is due next week, so the business knows they need to have the funds to pay it.

Cash flow can be forward projected for the next few days or for a number of weeks or months in advance. Cash flow projections can indicate a point in the future where there is a danger that your business could potentially run out of money. Knowing this, you can put strategies into place to prevent your business from running out of cash.

In the Business StartUp Resources Library, there is an extremely comprehensive webinar about cash flow and a downloadable template for a simple cash flow predictor. Find out more here: https://healthynumbers.com. au/members/product/business-startup-training/

Part of putting these strategies into practice means fostering a 'no waste' mindset.

It's really easy to waste money when getting started and it is also easy to spend money on the wrong things. However, even small amounts of money going out of your business will deplete your profit. When you set the example, then the rest of your team will follow.

The best way to prevent any money from inadvertently leaking out of your business is to identify any little holes that allow resources of any kind to be wasted. I'm not just talking about money here – although money is a key resource that you want to target for wastage prevention.

What sorts of things would you look for? Check all monthly recurring costs and ask yourself, 'Do I really use this?' 'Do I really need this?' and 'Am I paying the best price for what I use?'

When you are watching your costs, there is no room for paying 'just in case' money. You can always subscribe again in the future if you find you really do use the service.

If someone approaches you with advertising or marketing opportunities, take a good look at them before you commit. Ask yourself, 'How does this fit in with my overall marketing plan?' and 'Will this target my ideal client?'

It's really easy to waste time when you are in business. Every day, you need to ask yourself, 'Is what I'm doing the best use of my time?' Plan your month, your week and your days so that the time you spend doing what you do is for the best outcome for your business. You might enjoy posting on social media. The question is: how is that truly bringing you more clients?

There are many ways that a business can waste resources. When you identify one of your values as being 'no (or low) waste' you can make significant difference in your business, the impact you have in your community and your overall viability.

So, we've looked at some of the nitty-gritty, behind-the-scenes considerations such as structure, compliance and finance, after having taken the time to consider yourself, your idea, your clients and your brand. It's time to bring this all together and actually attract the business you need to be successful! You need a marketing plan.

7. YOUR MARKETING

'You can build the best mousetrap in
the world; if no one knows, they will not
beat a path to your door.'

RALPH WALDO EMERSON

alph Waldo Emerson is attributed with saying this chapter's quote,
but it's actually a misquote of the following: 'If a man has good corn
or wood, or boards, or pigs, to sell, or can make better chairs or knives,
crucibles or church organs, than anybody else, you will find a broad
hard-beaten road to his house, though it be in the woods.'

I first heard the mousetrap quote when I was studying marketing at
university. I actually prefer the real quote because it not only captures the
importance of marketing, it also emphases the quality of your offering.

Marketing is not just about Instagram and Facebook, although social
media can be an important part of your plan. For your business to be
successful, you need to do more. You need to create a marketing strategy.

When a business doesn't have a clear marketing strategy, it is distracted
by the latest, bright, shiny marketing or advertising initiative. This can lead
to wasted time, wasted money and, ultimately, damage to the image of the
business and its brand.

A couple of years ago, I started working with a chiropractor in North
Queensland. He told me he had just paid $2,000 for a road sign, one of those

large ones you see driving along the freeway. The sign was going to be located about 5km away on the way out of town. I asked him, 'Did the salesperson tell you the success rate of these signs?' and he asked me what I meant by that. What I meant was it would have been useful, based on previous experience, for the salesperson to have indicated how many new clients the chiropractor could expect from the sign. My client hadn't thought to ask. He told me how nice the sales guy was and that he'd said he'd help with designing the sign and put the chiropractor in contact with someone who could do a good job. This would be in addition to the $2,000 for the road sign.

If you were to spend $2,000 plus design costs on a sign, how many new clients would you expect to generate from that? For that much money, you would want to know that you would have a certain number of new clients. What would be the number to make the amount of advertising investment worthwhile?

The other question to ask in this scenario is: how does a road sign fit in with the brand and all the other aspects of the marketing plan?

There are a lot of people offering to do your marketing or teach you about marketing. They charge a lot of money for it, but there are two things to know about marketing your business in advance:

- There is no magic bullet.

- You need to stick with something for a period of time for it to work – consistency wins the race.

Having a marketing plan and implementing it step by step will get you the results that lead to business success. In this chapter, we're going to cover what marketing actually is, why it's important and create a client journey map. The end result will be a marketing plan you can measure results against.

WHAT IS MARKETING?

There are multiple ways to explain marketing. For me, marketing is really how you present yourself in the world with the intention to attract and retain your ideal clients.

Effective marketing does a series of things to help you grow your business:

- It helps your ideal clients to find you.

- It helps your ideal clients to identify why you are different to the competition, which helps them decide to work with you and not someone else.

- It helps build trust with your consumers.

- It creates and solidifies your business reputation in the marketplace and in your community.

You may offer the best service in the world, but no one will know unless you promote yourself.

Most people want to jump straight into social media: 'How do I best use Instagram? Facebook? Is Instagram better than Facebook?' Then they think: 'Do I need to send out a newsletter? Where should I advertise? How do I get found on Google?'

But an effective marketing strategy goes back to the beginning. In previous chapters we have identified:

- Who you are and what you do.

- Your competition – both direct and indirect.

- What makes you unique.

- Your ideal client.

- The true value of your offering.

- What feeds into your brand.

We will need all of these to build a marketing plan. And we need just one more tool in advance: the client journey map.

YOUR CLIENT JOURNEY MAP

A client journey map is just that – a map that a business creates to articulate the journey someone takes from knowing nothing about their business to the point where that person becomes a client. The journey then continues for the lifetime of the client/business relationship.

When I worked at Qantas, we ran a workshop and one of the segments was called 'Moments of Truth'. It was based on Jan Carlzon's work at Scandinavian Airlines. Jan Carlzon was the CEO and developed the concept in relation to exceptional customer service.

A moment of truth is any time a client has an interaction with your business. Today, we are more likely to call it a touch point or an interaction point. Whatever you call it, the impact is the same – it is the point where a client experiences engagement with your business. The client journey map is made up of all the touch points they might experience – all these moments of truth.

In the Qantas training program, we looked at all the touch points for a passenger on a journey from LA to Lizard Island (Qantas owned Lizard Island at the time). It would be tempting to think the journey starts at the airport, but the reality is that journeys like these start long before the passenger arrives at the check-in desk. There's research, planning, booking their travel and making arrangements and so on, all before they pack their bags and call a cab.

Google is constantly studying consumer habits. The company has discovered that most people aren't ready to buy at the first touch point. That seems obvious when you think about it. When we consider our own behaviour, most of us aren't ready to buy when we first hear about a product or service.

Google found, in its study, that a buyer needs seven hours of interaction across eleven touch points in four locations to make a purchasing decision.

This is why the client journey map is so important. It maps out the moments which add up to the amount of time your potential client spends with you before they start to buy from you. This also helps explain why it takes so long for some business startups to find a steady stream of new clients:

- They don't know what the touch points are for their clients.

- They don't know where their clients come from.

When you understand all the steps that your clients take in their decision-making process, this helps you put together your marketing plan. One of the key outcomes of your marketing plan is to take your clients from knowing nothing about you and your business to being an ongoing or repeat customer.

Activity: Client Journey Map

You can download a client journey map worksheet here: http://www.healthynumbers.com.au/book-templates

Take this worksheet and identify every single moment of truth where your clients may interact with your business. Add to it as you go through the next section on different aspects of marketing.

MARKETING CHANNELS

Marketing is concerned with the following:

- Advertising

- Public relations (PR)

- Promotions

- Sales.

Each of these can be handled online and offline. When it comes to marketing, both worlds are important.

ADVERTISING

There is almost no end to the available advertising options – online and offline. Almost everything you do is some form of advertising.

Google ads is the method you use to pay to appear on search results. You can buy space to display banners and websites that appear at the top of the page when someone uses a search engine. When someone searches a key word, there is a price attached to that word. The more popular words cost the most. The thing is, until you know what words your people are looking for, you could spend a lot of money on the wrong words. Google offers a way to search the popular search terms using its keyword planner. You can access this by going to https://adwords.google.com/KeywordPlanner.

To use the keyword planner, you need a Google AdWords account, which you would access through your Google account. Once you log in, you can then search for words you might use, and the keyword planner shows you the terms that people are using similar to the ones you have searched.

For example, say a hairdresser is a curl specialist and they enter 'curly hairdresser'. The Google keyword planner shows the following as similar search terms:

- Curly hair products

- Curly hairstyles

- Best products for curly hair

- Best curly hair products

- Hair products for curly hair

- Hairstyles for curly hair

The keyword planner then shows the volume of times the term has been searched and the amount that each click would cost if the hairdresser were to buy that term.

In contrast, *Search engine optimisation (SEO)* is the process of getting traffic from the free, organic, editorial or natural search results on search engines. When we talk about SEO being 'free', what it refers to is unpaid advertising from a search engine point of view. It is far from free when considered from a business point of view. It costs a lot to have your website optimised and to keep up to date with the key search terms – again, if you don't know which words are important, effort in terms of time and money can be wasted.

Facebook advertising might work for a business that has broader reach, such as an online clothing store. I have a friend who is a sucker for Facebook advertising. She'll be sitting on her couch watching TV and checking Facebook during commercials, and when an ad for a low-cost item shows up in her feed, she admits she thinks 'I've worked hard today, I deserve this.' Facebook ads may also work to attract people to take up a special offer. For example, a free webinar or a white paper offered on Facebook might generate interest for a business.

At the time of writing, Instagram doesn't have advertising, although the word is out that there will be advertising available there soon. LinkedIn also has advertising options.

It can be both very complex and very expensive to get your online advertising to give you the results you want in terms of new clients. My experience with many businesses is that it can take time to figure out the best way to use advertising on social media platforms. It's best to take a small amount of money and advertise every day, then track the results and tweak the ads to gain more traction. Over time, you'll figure it out. Every business is slightly different. There is no magic wand, unfortunately.

What are the offline options? Now, let's enter the physical world of advertising.

Print ads can be taken out in magazines, newspapers, the local paper, your local school magazine and so on.

Letter box flyer drops might attract your ideal clients and be more cost effective than any other advertising. I have seen this be particularly effective when the letter boxes in a certain area are selected. Certainly don't add to letter boxes already bulging with junk mail. If your flyer includes the offer: 'Bring this flyer to receive your introductory session', this is actually an example of advert and promotion combined – a promotion being a special offer. The reason you tell the client to bring the flyer is that it helps you track that the flyer has done its job.

Posters in community areas can be especially effective for a business wanting to attract locals, such as a children's dance studio, or a new flower shop or yoga studio.

Signage is very important. One of the things I always suggest to my clients is to watch what other people are doing. Not in order to copy, but to trigger ideas.

PUBLIC RELATIONS

This is anything that adds to the professional maintenance of the favourable public image of your business. This could be pretty much anything. You might be the sort of person who is involved in your community and that will reflect in your business. You might sponsor local sports events.

I work a lot with dentists and some of them really like to go into the schools to provide education about the importance of oral hygiene and cleaning teeth. Yes, it might bring some new patients – but it is mostly their way of being part of their community and educating people about how to achieve good oral hygiene.

There are companies that charge a lot of money to generate PR for businesses. I suggest you look for ways to do it naturally and organically. It can cost a lot of money with very little return.

Trust me – there will be people trying really hard to sell you SEO, Google, social media and PR services. Be extremely cautious of people who promise the world. It's important to track and measure success.

PROMOTIONS

Having a promotion can be a good way to get people to give you a try. Then, once someone has been a customer once, your job is to help them become a loyal customer.

This is an important statistic to track. For every person who comes in with a promotion, track how many return and become ongoing clients. Tracking the patterns of behaviour of your clients will tell you a lot about them and about your business.

Look around at what others do in the way of promotions – again not to copy, but to be inspired by what they are doing.

SALES

Sales is a system and there are multiple processes that sit within it. Some people are better at sales than others.

One of the important things for you to consider in your business as you get started is: will it be easy for my customers to buy from me?

Think about when you try to buy something. When it is easy to purchase, are you more or less likely to buy? If it is difficult to make the purchase, are you more likely or less likely to buy?

Businesses with online stores that report high abandon rates are always looking for ways to make it easier for customers to buy online.

As part of your client journey map, you will identify the purchase points and how the client gets to these points. One of the best ways to gain sales experience if you have never been in a situation or a role where you have had to sell anything is to take a job working in sales. I personally never had to sell anything prior to starting my own business. When a friend of mine asked me to help him out at the markets, it was such a learning experience for me. I also took a job in retail and worked in a café so I could understand what it felt like to sell to customers. I even joined a network marketing group – this was about the hard sell and not at all for me. What each of these and a few other experiences taught me has been invaluable in forming my own sales system.

Here are a few sales tips you might find useful:

- It's always about understanding your customer's problem and truly wanting to solve it.

- It helps to find ways to make an immediate personal connection – both online and offline. One of the best ways to make an immediate personal connection with a customer is eye contact, a smile and a 'Hello.' In the virtual world, there are a number of ways to connect. If someone comments or likes your photos or posts, always say, 'Thank You.' If you don't know what to say in words, emojis are a great standby. A smiley face can be the perfect response.

- If you have a business where people call you, always ask for their name and contact details – their number, at least – so you can contact them to follow up when they have had time to think about it.

■ It's always good to ask any new client, 'How did you hear about us?' This helps you know which advertising or promotion campaigns are effective.

■ It's great to ask: 'Has some one referred you to us?' Referrals are an extremely powerful way to build your business.

There are businesses that pride themselves on never having spent a single cent on external advertising – they've grown their entire business through referrals. I use an online IT service for my WordPress site and it's an example of such a business. There are numerous specialty service providers who have done the same thing.

Referrals are probably one of the most important aspects of marketing. Who might refer to you? I always say to my clients, 'Who else has your people?' If Karen is your ideal client, then where else does Karen go? What other businesses or groups does Karen spend time with? If you build a relationship with them, they may refer their clients to you.

I can't stress enough the importance of word-of-mouth referrals. In general, people buy from people they know, like and trust. The Google study showed that it takes seven hours and eleven touch points for a person to decide to purchase. Referrals is how we fast track that process.

Recently, a very good friend of mine recommended a new physiotherapist. I called and made an appointment. I did no research; I just booked. I didn't even have an idea how much she would charge – it was totally irrelevant. For me, the person making the recommendation said, 'This physiotherapist is great,' and I totally trusted the judgement and experience of my friend. It helped that the physio was located two suburbs from my home, but I would have been prepared to travel much further.

People do this all the time, tending to value the opinion of friends or trusted providers they already have a relationship with over anything a business might say about themselves. If you identify and build a relationship with a few trusted people who go on to recommend your business to their clients, you could ultimately create a referral-based business.

With all this in mind, it's time to establish your marketing plan.

PUTTING TOGETHER A MARKETING PLAN

Your first question might be: what does a marketing plan even look like?

There are numerous ways to document your marketing efforts. I remember Maggie Beer, the famous Australian chef, telling a group at a lunch I attended that her marketing plan was written on the back of an envelope. I suggest a little more structure than that, but it just goes to show!

Here's the template that I work through with clients:

Activity: Marketing Plan

You may want to download your own marketing plan template at: http://www.healthynumbers.com.au/book-templates.

You can then work through each aspect of your marketing plan as you read the rest of this section.

The first page pins down elements we've already been through, so you can write up the notes you've made already into your template.

- Your ideal client

- Your value proposition

- The client service you offer

Then we move to your marketing goals – the things you want to achieve in your business.

You may have heard of the SMART acronym in relation to goal setting:

Specific and simple – keeping it specific and simple keeps us focused.

Measurable – measuring success is how we know whether our goal has been achieved.

Attractive – goals must be appealing and not just in the short term; long term is important.

Realistic – goals need to be achievable in order for them to motivate us.

Time based – we need to indicate when goals will be achieved by.

Here are some poor examples of marketing goals:

- I want to see more clients.

- I want to rank number one in a Google search.

- I want more Facebook likes, Instagram followers and so on.

Each of the above are too broad. They don't clearly convey:

- How many more clients you want.

- Why you want to rank number one in a Google search for.

- How many likes and shares you want. What ratio of conversion? What level of engagement?

Here are some examples of well-defined goals:

- From day one, I want to build a business where for every three enquiries I receive, two of them are from referrals.

- We need to generate 100 website hits that lead to twenty enquiries that lead to five new clients every quarter. (This would be based on your knowledge that for every twenty potential clients who come along, you know five will become clients. And in order to get twenty enquiries, you know you need 100 website hits. This is an example only. You would develop this marketing data for your business over time.)

- For every three new clients we gain, two become repeat, loyal customers. (One of the goals I always encourage my clients to have is in regard to client retention. There is so much focus on getting new clients. I truly believe that if you have a marketing goal that focuses on client retention, it makes a difference to the numbers of clients that keep coming back to you. This takes the pressure off always having to find new clients.)

These sorts of goals give you something to work with in your marketing plan.

Let's see if my first example passes the SMART test:

Specific = two out of three enquiries comes from referrals.

Measurable = two out of three enquiries.

Attractive = this certainly sounds like an attractive business goal.

Realistic = Totally possible.

Time = From the start of the business.

With goals like this, you can start to map out actions to take to reach these goals – step by step by step (we'll get to this on page 4 of the plan).

The next page of the marketing plan concerns how to track results. You've set your goals; now, how will you know if you have achieved them? You set measures that track your success.

Using our previous example, for every three enquiries I receive, I want two of them to be from referrals. The measures would be:

- Number of new clients each month.

- Number of new clients who come from referrals.

Knowing these two measures would then let you calculate whether two out of three new clients are coming from referrals.

It's important to measure results so that you gain an appreciation for what works and the results you achieve from your marketing efforts. Measures help you to make informed decisions. What else would you measure? I recommend limiting it to a few key metrics, focusing on the ones related to your business and marketing goals.

For example:

- How many new clients each month/week.

- Average spend of a customer.

- How clients find out about you.

- The cost of acquiring a new client.

- Client retention (monthly/quarterly) – this is an important measure as it can alert you if you are losing clients.

- Social media engagement.

When it comes to social media, it's really easy to be seduced by vanity metrics – the large number of likes, followers, shares you generate, as mentioned in Chapter 4. They can be easily manipulated but do not necessarily correlate to sales and profit. They might make you feel good, but they are often not a true indicator of business success. You'll see other businesses and people with thousands or tens of thousands of followers, and there will be a part of you that wants to be like them. You'll like everything they do, follow them and maybe aspire to have them follow you. However, engagement is much more important than likes and followers. Having fifty people truly engaged every day is more powerful than having ten thousand followers who are not engaged at all.

What might true engagement look like in your business? There are three main categories of engagement:

- **Conversation:** This is the two-way flow between you and your audience. Replying to the content of others and getting responses to your content is the basis of any social network. If your competitors aren't responding to people, it's a great opportunity to be relevant and fill the void. This will attract an audience who are already interested in what you have to say.

- **Amplification:** If the content is compelling, it is shared around the globe quickly via various social media platforms.

- **Applause:** This is the most passive action on social media; it is the community saying it cares. The algorithms on Likes for Facebook and Instagram help directly by getting posts seen by more people; a Like is a vote for your content and signals to others that you're an authority on the topic.

When you measure the behaviour of your clients, you understand what to do more of and where to stop spending valuable resources. Numbers tell you the story.

So You Want to Start a Business™		HEALTHY NUMBERS		So You Want to Start a Business™		HEALTHY NUMBERS
Measures to Track Results				**Actions to Achieve Results**		
Goal 1	1			Goal 1	1	
	2				2	
	3				3	
Goal 2	1			Goal 2	1	
	2				2	
	3				3	
Goal 3	1			Goal 3	1	
	2				2	
	3				3	

It's best to set just one or two marketing goals to start with. I certainly suggest no more than three. Once you have your goals and have identified the measures to track them, it's time to think about the broad actions you need to take to achieve these goals. This is page 4 of your marketing plan template.

For example, your goal is, say, three new clients every month. Ask yourself:

- What do you know about where your clients come from? This is the information in the client journey map.

- Do they come from word-of-mouth referrals? Do they come from Facebook? Instagram? Other social media? Do they come from your website?

If your clients mostly come from word-of-mouth referrals from other local businesses, one of your actions might be to connect with these local businesses. If your people are more likely to come from Instagram, your action would be to design and implement an Instagram campaign. This might include learning how to use Instagram most effectively and following others who are reputed to embrace best practice, for inspiration. If you use Facebook or Instagram, do you know what the ratio of likes is to new clients signing up for your services or buying your products?

The thing I've found with any number of the business owners I've worked with over the past twenty-plus years – small business, solo operator and large corporate – is this: most people's gut feel for the numbers turns out to be wrong! People usually overestimate and exaggerate the case. This is why it is so important to measure the actual behaviour of your clients as you go. One of the reasons this happens is that most of us have a confirmation bias. We find evidence to support what we believe. That is, we believe what we want to believe. Over the past few years, I have worked with many health professionals, personal trainers, yoga instructors, Pilates instructors, dentists, physiotherapists and more. When we discuss client retention, so many of them believe – based on their gut feel – that they have ninety per cent client retention. When we start to look at the data, we often find that the client retention is much less than they 'feel' it is. There is a large number of clients who no longer attend classes, sessions or appointments, and the business doesn't even realise. It's important to track the numbers.

Page 5 in the marketing plan provides a one-year overview. I encourage my clients to use this to mark in events for the whole year – school holidays, Easter and other public holidays, Valentine's, spring, winter solstice – anything that you believe will be important to your business. This is especially useful to identify major events that you may want to participate in during the year, and periods that will have an impact on your business. For example, some businesses are most affected by school holidays, public holidays or large national events.

So You Want to Start a Business™   HEALTHY NUMBERS

One Year Overview

January	February	March	April

May	June	July	August

September	October	November	December

You can use this page to list various activities and events that are important to you, across the year or that will in some way impact your business. For example Easter, Valentine's Day, school holidays, Christmas and any other industry specific events |

The reason this groundwork is so important is that it creates the structure for your marketing plan and it helps to ensure that all your efforts bring about great results. There will always be the temptation to jump onto Instagram and post some lovely images, or run some Facebook posts, or draft and send out a newsletter by email. Trust me, these efforts will be more powerful if they are part of your overall marketing strategy rather than random attempts to get attention.

Pages 6–9 of the marketing plan are there for you to map out more detailed initiatives for each of the months of the year.

So You Want to Start a Business™   HEALTHY NUMBERS

Marketing Initiatives Per Quarter

Quarter 1 Initiatives

Initiative	January	February	March
e.g. Instagram			

Pages 10–12 offer templates for detailed action plans to help you get really specific about the actual tasks required, resources needed, responsibilities involved and the deadline.

So You Want to Start a Business™

Detailed Action Plans

Initiative	

Goal	

Tasks	Resources Needed	Responsibilities	Deadline

You can see below an example of an initiative – create and distribute flyer. There are many tasks involved in this one simple initiative:

So You Want to Start a Business™			HEALTHY NUMBERS
Detailed Action Plans Date: 25 April 2017			
Initiative	create and distribute flyer		
Goal	have 20 clients – at least – in the studio every month by 25 November 2017		
Tasks	**Resources Needed**	**Responsibilities**	**Deadline**
Draft Design for the brochure	Wording What size brochure? Research other brochures Logo, business specs sheet	Karen Josh	5 May
Research graphic designer	Upwork	Karen	5 May
Create client journey map for brochure	Client Journey Map template	Josh and Karen	8 May
Distribution	How far to distribute? Create plan Find brochure deliverers	Steve	10 May

At different stages in your business, there will be a different focus in your marketing plan. When you get started, there will be some basics:

■ Website.

■ Social media presence – deciding which social media platforms to use and what purpose they serve in your business; for example, engagement, retention, lead generation, attracting people to your website. This was covered in detail in Chapter 4: Your brand.

- Physical presence – signage, brochures and so on.

Essentially, your marketing plan gives you the answers to the questions that you need to think about every day. What am I doing to get more clients? What am I doing to ensure the ones I have keep coming back?

Marketing is one of the most important systems in your business. Without marketing, you will find it difficult to attract any new clients. Without a marketing plan, your efforts will be haphazard and you could potentially waste a lot of resources: time, money and energy. Badly executed marketing plans could even damage your brand.

In contrast, well-executed marketing campaigns can truly set you apart in your industry. Having worked through this chapter, you'll have a client journey map and marketing plan that form a solid foundation for promoting your business.

CONCLUSION: RUN WITH IT!

'Dear optimist, pessimist, and realist – while you guys were busy arguing about the glass of wine, I drank it! Sincerely, the opportunist!'

THE 'QUEEN OF QVC', LORI GREINER,
WHO JOINED THE ABC SHOW
SHARK TANK IN 2012 ALONGSIDE BARBARA CORCORAN

Most people have lost touch with what it takes to create a really successful business. There are stories in the media that would have us believe that it is easy to create a business that can be sold off to one of the giant companies for many millions. But if it is so easy, why isn't everyone doing it?

What we don't hear about are the entrepreneurs toiling away for many years and the numbers of failed prototypes along the way. Angry Birds was Rovio's fifty-second game. James Dyson went through 5,126 attempts before perfecting his revolutionary Dyson vacuum cleaner. Groupon nearly went completely bankrupt before it soared to dizzying heights.

It is human nature to gravitate to the success stories, and it is these stories that inspire and motivate us to create our own businesses. Mostly we only hear part of the story. The person who goes from $0 to six or seven figures in just eight months! The backstory is that they had exceptional experience from years of working in a similar industry and were able to bring along a database of potential clients that immediately guarantee the volume of work to generate that level of income. It would have been incredible had they not been an overnight success!

Another scenario I have observed goes as follows ... A business starts in June 2005 and from then until 2011, it really is on struggle street: there is little or no money, very few clients, the business gives the product away for free, and the owners eat one-minute noodles and sleep under the desk. Late 2011, they start to make money and in 2015, they float on the stock exchange for millions of dollars. The success story is reported in the media as the time from 2011 to 2015. For some reason, the story of that journey from to June 2005 to 2011 becomes invisible. Another overnight success story.

Here is what I have learned in the past ten years of being in my own business, working with people in their own businesses and studying, reading about and listening to business owners and entrepreneurs: overnight success is more likely to be the exception than the rule. For the vast majority of people who create their own business, success requires working longer and harder than they have ever worked before. If you are thinking, 'That's okay with me – I work hard now; it can't be any worse than my current job,' you might be in for a surprise.

The early years can be tedious, boring, worrying and exhausting – remember, you will mostly be doing everything yourself, and there may be very little income to start with. For the majority of businesses, success is a marathon, not a sprint. Often, the first few years are spent building and laying the foundations with little fanfare, few accolades and not a lot of money.

And the 'lucky break' might never happen. Some years ago, I had a client who had an amazing business making specialised children's clothing. We had been working together for a few months when she announced that this was all too hard. She wanted to know, 'When do I get my lucky break?' I was curious about what she meant. It turns out that she was friends with Heidi Middleton and Sarah-Jane Clarke who founded Sass and Bide. She was waiting for the same kind of lucky break she believed they had when they met Sarah Jessica Parker, which resulted in their being commissioned to make one-off pieces for the show *Sex and the City*. The resulting publicity from the opportune product placement is believed to have contributed to the brand's meteoric rise in popularity.

My client subsequently gave up her business idea and accepted a part-time position in a design company. 'Easier than doing everything myself,' she said. At least she tried. I believe that her business was as viable as Sass and Bide. She was banking on overnight success and hoping a lucky break would land in her lap. The thing is, it's called a lucky break for a reason. 'Luck is what happens when preparation meets opportunity,' as the Roman Philosopher Seneca said.

This book is all about setting solid foundations for the future success of your business. If you are keen to grow your business to be the next Sass and Bide or the equivalent in your business sector, it's important to remember that explosive growth can also cause unexpected problems. If a business is not prepared with a strong team, solid foundations and an ability to scale, being an overnight success could lead to the end of the business. A website that has a meltdown, an inability to service the demand for products or services, and major cash flow issues are just a few of the potential things that happen when a business grows faster than expected. A business that can cope with increased demand takes time and experience to develop.

While the idea of overnight success might seem appealing right now as you dream of creating your business, remember: slow and steady wins the race. This journey is all about making the right choices every day, over and over again.

In this book, I have outlined the seven elements necessary to create a successful business.

The first chapter focused entirely on you and what sort of person it takes to be in business. It helped explain what you are really getting into when you start a business and provided ways to assess if you really have what it takes to be successful with your own startup.

The second chapter was all about your idea. Ultimately, it asked: is there anyone out there who wants your idea enough to pay actual money for it? This chapter helped you to explore what your idea really is, what value you provide, and whether your idea is viable.

Chapter 3 was all about your clients. Having a great idea is one thing; it's the people who will pay for it who are really important. Who are these people? This chapter asked how much you know about them and how much you need to know about them so that you can: (1) find them; and (2) tell them about your idea.

Chapter 4 was dedicated to your brand and what that means as a small business. More and more, your clients are looking to you to be different and to stand for something. This chapter helped you understand what is necessary to create and promote your brand.

Chapter 5 focused on structure and compliance matters. These may not be the most exciting aspects of starting and running a business, however this chapter was extremely important. Which structure will work best for what you want from your business? This chapter highlighted the importance of understanding insurance, risk management and why you need systems and processes in your business.

Of course, one of the reasons we start a business is to make money. Chapter 6 was all about the business finances. This chapter helped you understand how much money you need to get started, how to calculate your break-even point, and how to be clear about the difference between profit and revenue. There was also a terrific section dedicated to improving cash flow. Running out of money is the number one reason that most businesses fail.

The seventh element to running a successful business is marketing. You've figured out who your client is (Chapter 3) and you've established your brand (Chapter 4). Marketing is all about attracting and retaining your clients. This chapter addressed the importance of taking the time to develop a solid marketing plan. This is what gives you clear direction and places you ahead of many other businesses.

Chris Hadfield is a Canadian astronaut. His biography is full of stories about the ways he prepared himself for opportunity. One of my favourite stories is actually not even about space. He was taking part in a Canadian Air Show when he realised that an Elton John concert was taking place nearby at the same time. He bought tickets and wondered, if he had the chance to play on stage with Elton, what song he would play. There's only one possible song that an astronaut would play with Elton John – 'Rocket Man'. So Chris practised Rocket Man on his guitar, just in case, just on the off chance that he might get to play on stage with Elton John. If the opportunity presented itself, he was ready!

Thank you for choosing to read my book and spend this time with me. This book was written for you, someone who wants to start a business of your own, so that, like Chris Hadfield, you can be as prepared as possible for all the opportunities that come your way.

You may like to go back to Chapter 1 and review the section entitled 'Why?' and reflect on why *you* really want to start a business.

I truly wish you every success and I would love to hear how things go – do please drop me a line!

Ingrid Thompson

Ingrid@healthynumbers.com.au

FREE GIFT FOR YOU

A big Thank You for purchasing this book!

As a gift I would like to give you all of the referenced templates throughout the book – 100% Free.

Simply visit www.StartaBusinessTemplates.com for instant access. You will be asked for your name and email address so that we can continue to send you updates as they happen.

REFERENCES

'If you are not willing to learn, no one can help you.
If you are determined to learn, no one can stop you.'

ZIG ZIGLAR

Throughout this book I have referred to some of the books I have read and that have had their impact on what I know about business and about life.

Here is a list of some of the books that I have read, some multiple times. I often return to favourite sections or chapters.

You may like to read some of these, and certainly I would encourage you to create our own collection of books.

Podcasts are also a terrific way to find out more about what is going on in the business world and I have listed a few of my favourites. Again, I would suggest you explore the world of podcasts and create your own preferred listening list.

BOOKS

Carlson, Jan (1989), *Moments of Truth*

Covey, Stephen (1989), *The 7 Habits of Highly Effective People*

Furr, Nathan and Ahlstrom, Paul (2015), *Nail It, Then Scale It*

Gerber, Michael (1995), *The E-Myth Revisited*

Godin, Seth (2003), *Purple Cow*

Hadfield, Chris (2015), *An Astronauts Guide to Life on Earth*

Huffington, Ariana (2015), *Thrive*

Isaacson, Walter (2011),*Steve Jobs*

Lewis, Michael (2016), *The Undoing Project*

Priestley, Daniel (2013), *Entrepreneur Revolution*

Ries, Eric (2011), *The Lean StartUp*

Roosevelt, Eleanor (1960), *You Learn by Living*

Sinek, Simon (2011), *Start with Why*,

Stewart, Martha (2005), *The Martha Rules*

PODCASTS

Just head over to iTunes and search for the following podcasts.

'Entrepreneurs on Fire', John Lee Dumas

'Unemployable', Brian Clarke

'Side Hustle School', Chris Guillebeau

'Flying Solo', Robert Gerrish

'Miss Bossy Boots', Stacey Morgan & Jane Hillsdon

'So You Want to Start a Business', Ingrid Thompson

ACKNOWLEDGEMENTS

Thank you to everyone who has been part of writing this book with me. It has been quite a journey. Some of you may not even know how much you have helped, quietly from the sidelines.

Thank you to my mum for instilling in me a love for books, an inquisitive mind and an ability to keep going when things just don't go the way I thought they might. At eighty-six years of age, Bette continues to inspire me every day. Thank you to my sister Lisa, for always believing that I am so much more than I think I am and for always backing even my strangest life choices. To my dad I am grateful for my genetic predisposition for and love of processes, systems, rituals and habits. Thank you to Des, who had a level of patience in his everyday actions that I can only continue to aspire to have myself. And thank you to my aunt Vera, a woman who has faced more challenges than any one human being ought to be asked to cope with in one lifetime and remains one of the happiest people I know. Vera is my inspiration, especially on days when I feel I might just give up.

Thank you to my many valued clients. I learn so much from you as we work together to create, start and grow your businesses. Some of you are mentioned in this book, but you all know who you are. I thank you for everything you have taught me about creating, starting and growing in business.

Sara Litchfield, my editor, I cannot thank you enough for taking my words and ideas and making them read in a way that just makes them so much more readable for everyone. Jacqui Pretty for your professional enthusiasm for this book, the ideas and the potential for a larger audience. The team at Morgan James I thank you for inviting me to be part of the Morgan James family.

To my dear friends who have read various versions and added comments, thank you. To my friends who have asked for updates, enquiring 'How is that book going?' – you just don't know how much those five little words have meant to me over the months. To the people who paid for advanced copies, some as long as two years ago, I know who you are and your copy is on its way.

My closest friends Christine and Kathryn and my sister Lisa, I'd like to thank you for saying to me independently and within a few hours of each other, 'What exactly do you do, Ingrid?' This was the wake-up call I needed to get really clear about who I am here to work with, who needs my help and who will gain the most from my expertise and experience. The answer to those questions has led me to write this book and so much more.

To my terrific Virtual Assistant and friend Annette, having you to help me and to keep me on track has made a huge difference to my business.

All three of our cats have been part of this book – Mousee, Mischa and Ollie – whether contentedly sleeping on the chair beside me, walking over the keyboard, or demanding attention when all I seemed interested in doing was watching the screen and pecking at the keyboard.

And, finally, thank you to the wonderful Mark, who is one of the nicest and smartest people I know. It's not easy living with someone who has a brain on fire with multiple thoughts from first light most mornings. Thank you for listening to every idea, whether at the beach, in a wine bar or on holidays – when you would rather be having a relaxing time. Thank you for reading every word of this book through all the edits, and for so much more.

ABOUT THE AUTHOR

Ingrid Thompson is the Founder of Healthy Numbers – a training and coaching business that helps people create, start and grow their own businesses.

With a Bachelor of Commerce majoring in business from the University of Queensland, Ingrid started out working in large corporations as a management accountant, a role she really loved. An opportunity to move from accounting into training and development was a major career shift and led to Ingrid studying for a Diploma in Adult Learning before completing a Masters in Coaching Psychology.

When it came time to leave the corporate world, Ingrid returned to accounting as an outsourced CFO for Small and Medium Businesses. In doing so, she found the people she most enjoyed working with; people running and growing their own business.

Since starting Healthy Numbers in 2003, Ingrid has worked with almost 1,000 businesses across a range of industries – health and wellness, travel, manufacturing, retail, clothing, real estate and more. As well as working with people to create, start and grow their businesses, she has helped a number of businesses scale and negotiate the sale of their business. She has even saved a few people from bankruptcy.

Ingrid hosts a popular podcast, 'So You Want to Start a Business', and has developed an online program of the same name. She had also created a niche program, 'So You Want to Start a Pilates Business', specifically for Pilates instructors and other movement professionals who are keen to open their own studio.

Ingrid lives in Sydney with her partner and their three, some times four, cats. She likes wine, yoga, sunshine, surfing and a "good murder mystery" or thriller - although perhaps not all at the same time.

ABOUT HEALTHY NUMBERS AND ADDITIONAL RESOURCES

I f you would like more ideas and assistance, we have a ton of resources over at www.healthynumbers.com.au.

More specifically, visit my Business Startup Training Resources Library: https://healthynumbers.com.au/members/product/business-startup-training/.

Read my blog: www.healthynumbers.com.au/blog.

You may like to take our Business StartUp Readiness Assessment which is designed to let you know where you are on the StartUp Readiness Scale: www.healthynumbers.com.au/bsrq.

Join our Facebook page: https://www.facebook.com/GrowingBusinessesHealthier/.

The very best place to find me is on LinkedIn: www.linkedin.com/in/ingridthompson.

At any time you may want to send me an email: Ingrid@healthynumbers.com.au.

You can hear me live on my very popular podcast 'So You Want to Start a Business' on iTunes.

Through the online program, 'So You Want to Start a Business', I coach you through the seven elements in person and guide you, step by step, along the pathway to create, start and grow your own business. To find out more, visit: www.healthynumbers.com.au.

Morgan James
Speakers Group

We connect Morgan James published
authors with live and online events
and audiences who will benefit
from their expertise.

Printed in the USA
CPSIA information can be obtained
at www.ICGtesting.com
JSHW022330140824
68134JS00019B/1396